VOCABULARY

Laurie Bauer

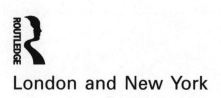

London and New York

First published 1998
by Routledge
11 New Fetter Lane, London EC4P 4EE

Simultaneously published in the USA and Canada
by Routledge
29 West 35th Street, New York, NY 10001

© 1998 Laurie Bauer

Typset in Times Ten and Univers by
Florencetype Limited, Stoodleigh, Devon

Printed and bound in Great Britain by TJ International Ltd.,
Padstow, Cornwall

British Library Cataloguing in Publication Data
A catalogue record for this book is available from the British Library

Library of Congress Cataloguing in Publication Data
Bauer, Laurie, 1949–
    Vocabulary / Laurie Bauer.
      p.   cm – (Language workbooks)
    ISBN 0–415–16398–6 (pbk.)
      1. Vocabulary–Problems, exercises, etc.   I. Title.   II. Series.
    PE1449.B348   1998
    428.1–dc21
    97-39921 CIP

ISBN 0–415–16398–6

For Keith and Ingrid

CONTENTS

USING THIS BOOK

Vocabulary is about words – where they come from, how they change, how they relate to each other and how we use them to view the world. You have been using words since before your second birthday to understand the wishes of others and to make your own wishes and feelings known. Here you will be asked to consider words in an objective manner – while remembering that objectivity should not exclude a certain amount of entertainment.

Chapters 1 and 2 provide some general background on the power and mystique of words and on the numbers of words we deal with in our everyday lives. One of the things about words is that we keep meeting new ones: as society changes we gain new words like *download* or *AIDS* and lose old ones like *barouche* or *reefer*. In Chapters 3, 4 and 5 we ask where the new words come from. Chapters 6 and 7 view words from two complementary angles: their meaning and their shape (shape being either their sound-shape or their spelling-shape). In Chapters 8 and 9 we go on to see how different words are used in different contexts and to try to work out the meanings of some of the very technical words we find in English. In Chapters 10 and 11 we look at the origins of words and how words change their meanings. And in Chapter 12 we take a brief look at dictionaries, the ultimate word-books.

All of this is an attempt to give you some kind of over-view of the fascination of words. But in a book of this size, it must be recognised that not everything can be covered. Some of the points which are not fully discussed in this book are covered – or are covered in more detail – in other books in the same series. Richard Hudson's book on *Word Meaning* and Richard Coates's on *Word Structure* deal in much more detail with things which are mentioned here, but about which a great deal more might be said. I do not here look at words as markers of regional identity (where does someone who calls a young cat a *kittling* come from?), at place names or personal names, at the skills required for word-games, or at the ways in which words are stored in the brain ready to be used at a moment's notice. Perhaps when you have read this book, you will be ready with a host of such questions to answer in further study.

ACKNOWLEDGEMENTS

I should like to thank Dick Hudson, the series editor, for his help in bringing this book into being, the Routledge team for their technical expertise, including that of their student reader, and my family for support. Especially I should like to thank Keith for being a guinea-pig, and Winifred for her much-appreciated and invaluable assistance.

The author and publishers would also like to thank the following for permission to reproduce copyright material:

The extract from The *International Express* article on page 2 is reprinted courtesy of Express Newspapers Plc.

The *Evening Post* article on page 3 is reprinted with kind permission of Wellington Newspapers Ltd.

'Ode to the Four-letter word', by Ogden Nash on page 3, © Estate of Ogden Nash, is reprinted by permission of Curtis Brown Ltd.

The article on page 5 is published with the permission of The *National Business Review*.

The article on page 20, © The *Australian* 1997 is reprinted with kind permission of The *Australian*.

The extract from *Fox in Socks* by Dr. Seuss on page 22, ™ and copyright © 1965 and renewed 1993 by Dr. Seuss Enterprises, L.P., is reprinted by permission of Random House Inc and Dr. Seuss Enterprises.

Extract from 'Life in the deep freeze' on page 45, © *Time* Magazine 1997, is reprinted with permission of Time Life Syndication.

The extract from *The Macquarie Concise Dictionary*, 2nd edn., 1988, on page 63, is reprinted by permission of the The Macquarie Library Pty Ltd.

THE MAGIC OF WORDS

1

In this chapter we look at the power of words. In particular we consider cases where words are thought of as being so powerful that they may not be uttered without fear of sanction.

There is a large amount of evidence which shows that people believe words to have magic powers. This is most easily illustrated with those very special words, people's names. In the traditions of modern Ethiopia, the real name of a child is concealed in case the child is bewitched through the use of the name. It is believed that knowledge of the name gives power over the person who bears that name. Beliefs of this type are widespread throughout the world. In Borneo, for example, the name of a sickly child is traditionally changed so that the spirits tormenting it will be deceived and leave the child alone. The spirits, apparently, can recognise people only by their names, not through other characteristics. An extreme example was reported by the early explorers in the Marquesas Islands. There it was possible for two people to exchange names as a sign of mutual respect. But this exchange of names also involved an exchange of responsibilities: obligations with respect to the family, friends and even enemies went with the change of name. A man might even be expected to go to war because of the responsibility to his new name.

In some cultures, the use of a particular name is an offence. In imperial China, for instance, it was a crime to use the name of a reigning emperor. This could provide problems when the emperor's name was also a common word. If this occurred in an English-speaking country today where the emperor's name was Bill, it would be illegal to talk about a bill from the electricity company, a bill before parliament or the bill of a bird. Similar prohibitions are found among the Zulus: there a woman is not allowed to utter the name of her husband or the names of his parents.

EXERCISE ✎

1.1 Can you think of any names that we are not supposed to mention or not supposed to mention outside certain specific contexts in any parts of the English-speaking world?

Similar kinds of constraints can apply to the names of things, as well as to the names of people. It is fairly common to find a taboo against the use of the name of a powerful animal such as a bear, tiger or crocodile. Instead phrases like 'honey-eater' or nick-names like 'Bruin' are used. In parts of Africa and India it is not done to name a snake. Instead you say things like 'There is a strap' or 'There is a rope.' It is believed that if you call something a snake it is likely to act like a snake, and bite you. In a similar vein, Bavarian farmers in Germany traditionally do not name the fox, in case using the word calls the fox, and causes it to attack their hens. In a very similar vein, we still say 'Talk of the devil', suggesting that speaking of someone causes them to appear. Finally, and more subtly, it used to be the case in China that a doctor who did not have the appropriate drug for his patient would write the name of the drug on a piece of paper, burn it, and get the patient to eat the ashes. It was believed that the name of the drug would be just as efficient as the drug itself.

One theory about the origin of these beliefs is that the magic of names is established as children learn language. As soon as small children learn the names for things, they can use those names and the item they name will appear – usually because some kind adult or older brother or sister fetches it. The link between saying the word and the appearance of the thing is a very strong one. Knowing the word is equivalent to having power over the object.

From our vantage point in twentieth-century 'civilised' society, we tend to be rather patronising about such irrational beliefs about names and words. We feel that we, as rational people, are not prone to them. We feel we know better. In fact nothing could be further from the truth. Innumerable instances can be found where people act as though the name of a thing has power equivalent to that thing.

EXERCISE ✎

1.2 Consider the following extract from an item that appeared in The *International Express* for 12–18 June 1996.

> Bosses have more than fifty ways of saying it, apparently, but they never use the word 'sack'. Rationalisation, re-engineering and organisational realignment are among euphemisms used, according to a union survey.
>
> Some workers soon to be jobless have been told: 'You've made yourself redundant', or 'This will get you out of a rut.'

How does this illustrate the power of the word?

The example cited in 1.2 raises another aspect of the magic of words. There are some words which are too forceful to be used in polite society. This is particularly the case, in English, for words denoting bodily functions. To a certain extent this is because the word reminds us too strongly of the action, and just as the action is not a public one, so too it is felt that the words should not be.

EXERCISE ✎

1.3 What makes people treat the words for private actions as private?

However, this is not the whole story, because if there are a number of words denoting the same thing, it is often possible to use some of them without causing offence (or at least, without causing as much offence). For example, small children can *pee*, *piddle* or *do a wee-wee*, and use the words in public without shocking anyone but the most prudish. In the hospital it is perfectly possible to speak of *urination* and *micturition* without giving offence. In informal contexts it is permissible to mention the need to *spend a penny* or *see a man about a dog* without risk of being thought coarse. But the contexts in which the word *piss* can be used are extremely limited. This prompted Ogden Nash to write:

> Ode to the Four-Letter Word
>
> When in calling, plain speaking is out;
> When the ladies (God bless 'em) are milling about,
> You may wet, make water or empty the glass;
> You can powder your nose, or the 'johnny' will pass.
> It's a drain for the lily, or man about dog
> When everyone's drunk, it's condensing the fog;
> But sure as the devil, that word with a hiss
> It's only in Shakespeare that characters - - - -.

An article showing the force of another common English word appeared in the Wellington newspaper *The Evening Post* on 20 December 1982. Part of that item is reproduced here:

> A complaint against the *New Zealand Times* of using obscene language has been dismissed by the Press Council.
> A Lower Hutt reader, Mr L. D. Leitch, complained to the council about the use of a word, 'a fairly widely used vulgarism for copulation', according to the council, in the paper's Bookworld column on September 5.
> The word appeared in a poem in an anthology of New Zealand verse reviewed by Michael King.
> Mr Leitch expressed dismay and disgust and asked the *New Zealand Times* to apologise.
> The paper's editor, Bob Fox, said the word was used

> in context where a qualified reviewer was discussing the latest addition to New Zealand literature.
>
> He said he would not have used it on the front page, but the word [appeared in] part of an arts page column, unadvertised, and was in context.
>
> It was not used in a prurient sense and was published after deep consideration in a newspaper which sought to cover literature with due seriousness.

The fact that the 'widely used vulgarism for copulation' is not used in the article reporting the case is just one of the things showing how powerful the magic associated with the word is. Others are the comment that it would not have been used on the front page, and that even so it was only published 'after deep consideration'. It is unlikely that there are many readers – if any – who have not heard the word *fuck*, which is presumably the 'vulgarism for copulation' in question. Neither does it seem that it is the naming of the act that is found distasteful, since the word *copulation* is used quite freely. *Fuck* is almost certainly a more common word than *copulate*, but because of the superstitious awe with which the word is viewed, papers cannot print it. Examples like this show clearly the power that some words have.

EXERCISES ✎

1.4 The example of *fuck* shows that the magic is connected with particular words rather than with the meaning of the word. Below are listed some concepts, for which you can probably think of a number of words. What synonyms can you find, and when would you use them? (You might like to consider what you would say in a court of law, to a doctor, in class, to your parents, to your friends.)

    to be intoxicated
    to evacuate the bowels
    to pass wind
    to die

1.5 We also show how powerful words are by using them to ward off ill luck. While many of these words indicate actions (like *touch wood*, for example), it is possible to use the words without the actions. What other examples of this behaviour can you find?

Perhaps one of the examples from the Christian tradition that most strongly indicates the power of words is the first line of the Gospel According to St John, where it is said that

> In the beginning was the Word, and the Word was with God and the Word was God.

However this is to be interpreted, it appears to be attributing divine characteristics to the word.

In all the examples that have been considered in this chapter it has been shown that words have a power of their own. This power might be considered magical in some cases. In other cases we might merely say that a person who can harness that power is talented or skilful. But even in our technological society, words continue to exert a very potent force on us. That is part of their fascination.

EXERCISE ✎

1.6 The following article appeared on page 6 of the New Zealand *National Business Review* number 519, for 21 March 1983. How does this article relate to what has been said in this chapter on the magic of words? What is your reaction to the facts in the article?

> FYI, verboten
>
> The Broadcasting Corporation last year handed down to its employees a stern list of words they were not allowed to utter on the air. But have you ever wondered what you're not allowed to say on a motor vehicle registration plate?
>
> Two letters on a car plate don't give much opportunity for unfortunate combinations; but with the three letter sequence on motorcycles, you have to be a bit more careful.
>
> A copy of the tender for the manufacture of plates has drifted into our hands, and the document spells it out.
>
> Single plates for motorcycles should run DPA through to QYK 'excluding the respective series FUC, FUK, FUX, FUZ (we have to remember that police and traffic officers will be riding a lot of these bikes), GOD, GUT, KOK, LOO, PEE, PIG (sensitive cops again), PIS, PIZ, POO (that's surely getting a bit *too* sensitive) and POX.'
>
> We think they've trapped anything that could possibly raise a blush on a meter maiden's (or traffic officer's) cheek. But if you do think of one that's been missed, don't tell us, tell the Post Office.

FOLLOW-UP READING

The examples of the magic of names in other cultures are taken from M. Leach (ed.), *Funk and Wagnalls Standard Dictionary of Folklore, Mythology and Legend* (New York: Funk and Wagnalls, 1972), B. Malinowski, *Coral Gardens and their Magic* (New York, etc.: American Book Company, 1935), E. B. Tylor, *Researches into the Early History of Mankind and the Development of Civilization* (Chicago and London: Chicago University Press, 1964. Revised and edited from the 1878 edition), and R. W. Williamson, *The Social and Political Systems of Central Polynesia* (Cambridge: Cambridge University Press, 1924). Of these, the Malinowski book, while very much more specific than the others, discusses the magic of words in an interesting way.

VOCABULARY
STATISTICS

2

In this chapter we consider some facts and figures about words, and why it is so difficult to be precise about these numbers.

How many words do you know? How many words did Shakespeare know? How many words are there in English, and how fast are we getting new ones?

These look like straightforward questions. When you realise that estimates of how many words an individual is likely to know vary between 3,000 and 216,000, it becomes clear that getting a satisfactory answer is not as straightforward as you might think. We need to think about why we should get such widely differing answers. Let's start with some of Shakespeare's words.

Look at the passage below, and decide how many words Shakespeare used to write this passage from *The Tempest* (V.i.88).

> Where the bee sucks, there suck I
> In a cowslip's bell I lie.

EXERCISE ✎

2.1 How many words do you think there are in this couplet?

You probably said that there are thirteen words in these two lines of Shakespeare's. However, you might have been a bit more precise and said that there are only twelve different words, because the word *I* occurs twice. But now think about the words *suck* and *sucks*. Do you want to say that because Shakespeare wrote these two different forms, it proves he knew two words? Or would you rather say that *suck* and *sucks* are, in some sense, the same word?

Word-form
Lexeme

The difficulty here is a terminological one. It seems contradictory to say both '*Suck* and *sucks* are two different words' and '*Suck* and *sucks* are the same word.' The apparent contradiction arises because we are using the word *word* in two different ways. With a bit of technical jargon we can solve the problem. We can say that *suck* and *sucks* are two different WORD-FORMS representing just one LEXEME. *Sucking* and *sucked* are other word-forms which also stand for the lexeme SUCK.

Now let us return to Shakespeare. When we ask how many words Shakespeare knew, are we interested in word-forms or lexemes? You will probably agree that we are more interested in lexemes. Yet the figures that are usually cited for Shakespeare's vocabulary, which credit him with knowing (or at least, having used – he probably knew a lot more, and seems to have invented a few!) about 30,000 different words, count word-forms rather than lexemes. If we counted lexemes, the result would be under 20,000.

EXERCISE ✎

2.2 Do any of the lexemes listed below have more word-forms than the lexeme GO? Do any of them have only one word-form? BE, CAT, CATCH, HAVE, IMPORTANT, MANY.

This is not the only problem we face in counting words. Consider the word *lie* in the couplet from *The Tempest*. The same form occurs in each of the following sentences, but you might not think that they are all the same lexeme:

(1) If I tell thee a lie, spit in my face (*Henry IV Pt 1*, II.iv)

(2) Who loves to lie with me? (*As You Like It*, II.v)

(3) I dare [. . .] spit upon him, whilst I say he lies (*Richard II*, IV.i)

If we look only at the form, we will not necessarily be able to tell how many lexemes are involved.

EXERCISE ✎

2.3 Can you see any reasons why we might want to say there is more than one lexeme LIE occurring in (1)–(3)?

Perhaps a bigger problem than all of these is how to treat compound words like *school-boy*. Some writers use a hyphen in such words, others use no space at all, others write them as two words. Not even English dictionaries can agree on how to write this and hundreds of other words like it. If we are making a list of English lexemes and we count *school-boy* simply as SCHOOL and BOY we find two lexemes.

But if we treat it as a new lexeme, perhaps writing it solid as *schoolboy*, we have the lexemes SCHOOL and BOY and the lexeme SCHOOLBOY as well. Counting compounds as new lexemes will mean that we end up with a much higher estimate of how many lexemes ordinary people know.

EXERCISE ✎

2.4 What is the smallest number of words and the largest number of words you could claim were illustrated in the following passage from *Love's Labour's Lost* IV.iii?

> They have pitch'd a toil: I am toiling in a pitch – pitch that defiles. Defile! A foul word. Well, 'set thee down sorrow!' for so they say the fool said, and so say I, and I am the fool. Well proved, wit. [. . .] O, but her eye! By this light, but for her eye, I would not love her – yes for her two eyes. Well, I do nothing in the world but lie, and lie in my throat. By heaven, I do love; and it hath taught me to rhyme, and to be melancholy; and here is part of my rhyme, and here my melancholy.

With all these problems – and a host of others that we have not considered – it is perhaps not surprising that it is very difficult to give an estimate of how many words people know. Even if we set out to test how many words you know, all the same problems would arise: how many different lexemes LIE do you know? should we count *schoolboy* as a new word? how many words do *suck* and *sucks* represent? should we count words not in dictionaries – such as names – as words?

Despite all this, there have been various attempts to test people's vocabulary to see how many words they know. These tests are usually done on the basis of dictionaries. If you read the blurbs on the dust jacket of several dictionaries in a book shop, they will probably tell you how many words they contain. What they will not tell you is how they counted. It's usually a fair bet that they have over-estimated to make the dictionary look as good as possible. But many tests have been made up, taking into account factors such as how frequently you are likely to have met certain words in texts, the numbers of words in dictionaries, and other factors. One such test is reproduced below.

EXERCISE ✎

2.5 Read through the list of words below, putting a tick next to words you know (words you could give a meaning for) and a question mark next to words you are not sure about. When you've been right through the list, go back and check the words you have marked with a question mark, to see if you can change them to ticks. Look at the five words with the highest numbers that you have ticked. Provide a synonym or definition of those five words, or show you know their meanings in some other way. Then check those meanings in a dictionary. (NB: You will need a *very* big dictionary for some of these words, or you may have to check in several dictionaries!) If you get more than one wrong, you need to go backwards through the list, repeating the procedure, until you can explain correctly four out of the five highest-numbered words with ticks. Count the words from the list that you have ticked up to the last correct tick, and multiply that number by 500.

1 as	11 abstract	21 aviary
2 dog	12 eccentric	22 chasuble
3 editor	13 receptacle	23 ferrule
4 shake	14 armadillo	24 liven
5 pony	15 boost	25 parallelogram
6 immense	16 commissary	26 punkah
7 butler	17 gentian	27 amice
8 mare	18 lotus	28 chiton
9 denounce	19 squeamish	29 roughy
10 borough	20 waffle	30 barf

31 comeuppance	41 cupreous
32 downer	42 cutability
33 geisha	43 regurge
34 logistics	44 lifemanship
35 panache	45 atropia
36 setout	46 sporophore
37 cervicovaginal	47 hypomagnesia
38 abruption	48 cowsucker
39 kohl	49 oleaginous
40 acephalia	50 migrationist

The number you get when you try exercise 2.5 will give you an estimate of the size of your vocabulary in line with the latest theoretical positions. But be careful with the figure! Do not try to compare your figure derived from this test with that provided by other people by other means. The number this test provides will be much lower than numbers provided by many other ways of estimating vocabulary size. Remember, too, that ideally you should do several such tests, and take an average of the results. And above all, remember that this test, like others, makes its own judgements about the kinds of question we have raised earlier.

Note that this test assumes that whoever you are, you will not have a vocabulary of more than 25,000 words. Only the most widely-read people will have a vocabulary even approaching that. If you ever get that far, you are unlikely to get there before your twenties, let's say twenty-two at the earliest. At the age of one and a half, the chances are that you knew under 300 words. A little arithmetic will tell you how many words you have to learn per year to achieve that total, and you can work out what that means in terms of words per day. To make the arithmetic simple, say that at one and a half you know 300 words, and at twenty-one and a half you know 20,300. That means 1,000 words per year, or three words a day on average. But you will not actually learn them at that average speed. For many years you will learn fewer than that average, and between the ages of eleven and eighteen you will learn more than that average. High school is all about learning words!

Other ways of counting words would make this total even more impressive.

EXERCISE ✎

2.6   Why do you think you learn most words in your teenage years? Do you think there are circumstances in which you might learn the words at some other period?

You should also note that the tests we have given are tests of your PASSIVE VOCABULARY, the words you recognise. Your ACTIVE VOCABULARY, or the words you use, will be smaller. When teachers tell you not to use the word *get* or to find a better adjective to replace *nice*, they are trying to encourage you to transfer words from your passive vocabulary into your active vocabulary.

Passive vocabulary
Active vocabulary

EXERCISE ✎

2.7   The following passage, from Chapter 14 of Jane Austen's *Northanger Abbey*, written in 1797 and first published in 1818, makes fun of people who use the word *nice* too often. Can you suggest more precise adjectives for the four examples that Henry gives?

> 'I am sure,' cried Catherine, 'I did not mean to say anything wrong; but it *is* a nice book, and why should not I call it so?'
> 'Very true,' said Henry, 'and this is a nice day, and we are taking a very nice walk, and you are two very nice young ladies. Oh! it is a very nice word indeed! – it does for every thing.'

Now you have some idea about how many words you actually know, but how many would you need to know before you could read a book or a newspaper? There are some children's books which use a very small vocabulary – no more than 300 words. But the children these books are aimed at know a lot more than 300 words, and the 300 words are not necessarily the ones which children would learn first. What is crucial is how common the words you know are.

Knowing the word *zygote* may be impressive, but it will not be very useful to you in everyday conversation. To carry out a normal conversation you need to know common words. For example, in most English texts, the word *the* alone will make up approximately 6 per cent of all the words you encounter. You need to understand *the* much more often than you need to understand *zygote*.

The Longman Dictionary of Contemporary English (*LDCE*), a dictionary written for people whose first language is not English, uses a set of 2,000 words to explain the words it lists. Sometimes it has to use a harder word, but it always marks such words so you can see what they are. This shows that you can write a large amount using just 2,000 words. In fact, it seems that if you know that many words, you can understand most of what you read except in the most difficult texts. Although the answer you get will depend on how you count words, it seems that knowing 2,000 words is likely to let you understand about 80 per cent of most texts. Knowing just 1,000 words will let you understand about 70 per cent of many texts. If you have been learning another language in school for five years, you probably know somewhere between 1,000 and 2,000 words of that language. In your first language you probably know that many words when you are about six.

EXERCISES ✎

2.8 In the last paragraph there are only two words (omitting the name *Longman*) which are not in the Longman list of 2,000 words used for definitions in the *LDCE*. Can you guess which they are, and can you suggest easier words to use instead of them?

2.9 To show you how much you can understand with just 2,000 words, all the words which are not on the Longman list in the following two brief texts have been replaced with nonsense forms. Can you reconstruct the originals? If one of the texts is more difficult to reconstruct than the other, why do you think this is so?

> For some creatures, such as small birds, sanglage cribement is a matter of life and death. If the feathers are allowed to become shankly, the bird will be disdaish to take off fast enough to avoid its cranles and will be disdaish to keep up its high body temperature if conditions become cold. Birds spend many hours bathing, clumming, oiling and walming themselves.
>
> (Desmond Morris, *The Naked Ape*
> (London: Corgi, 1967), p.174)

> It was July, and real July weather, such as they only had in old England. Everybody went bright brown like Red Indians with graming teeth and flashing eyes. The dogs moved about with their tongues hanging out, or lay

tergling in bits of shade, while the farm horses angived through their coats and menulated their tails and tried to kick the horse-flies off their barms with their great forse bounts.

(T. H. White, *The Sword in the Stone* (London: Fontana, 1938), pp. 10-11)

It will also have become clear to you in looking at some of the examples given here, that the most common words are, on the whole, rather short, while long words like *praetertranssubstantiationalistically* are very rare. The rule is not an absolute one. *Zo* is a very rare word, and *discouragement* is on the Longman list of 2,000 words, but there is nevertheless some truth to the generalisation. The very common words are articles (*a*, *the*), prepositions (*to*, *up*), demonstratives (*this*, *these*), pronouns (*he*, *she*) and auxiliary verbs (*am*, *have*, *can*) rather than nouns or verbs which, as a very rough and ready rule, tend to have more letters in them.

All this tells you about how many words you know and how many you need to know. But how many are there in English? The question is unanswerable because of the number of technical words for every conceivable specialist area from nuclear physics to stamp-collecting, from knitting to mechanical engineering. The question is also unanswerable because English keeps getting new words – probably in excess of 500 per year are deemed worthy of listing in major dictionaries. If all possible technical words are included, it seems likely that the total number of words of English exceeds one million.

FOLLOW-UP READING

Much of the information in this chapter, and in particular the test given in exercise 2.5, comes from Robin Goulden, Paul Nation and John Read 'How large can a receptive vocabulary be?' *Applied Linguistics* 11 (1990), pp. 341–363, where further similar tests can be found. David Crystal, *The Cambridge Encyclopedia of the English Language* (Cambridge: Cambridge University Press, 1995) also canvasses many of the same issues.

3

BORROWING

In this chapter we look at one way of getting new words: taking them from another language. We ask what kinds of words are 'borrowed' in this way, and whether there are types of words which cannot be borrowed.

In this chapter and the next two we will look at ways in which languages can get new words. We will be concerned with two fundamental ways of getting new vocabulary: either words are taken from another language (which is the subject of this chapter) or words are made up from a language's native resources (which will be the subject of the next chapters).

Borrow
Loan-word

When one language takes a word from another one, it is usually said to BORROW the word, and the word is called a LOAN-WORD. The terms are actually very inappropriate in this context. If you borrow a pen from someone, then that pen starts off as being their property and goes back to being their property when you have finished with it, with you having control of it in the meantime. If French borrows the word *tennis* from English, English still keeps the word and French will probably never 'give it back'.

In some cases a word which has been borrowed is returned, but usually in a rather different guise, and still without the original borrowing language losing it. For example, the English word *realise* was originally borrowed from French in the sixteenth century with the meaning 'make real'. In this sense it is possible to speak of realising plans or dreams, for instance. The meaning gradually changed in English, because *realise* was used to mean 'to apprehend with the clearness or detail of reality' (as the *Oxford English Dictionary* phrases it), and so the modern meaning of *realise* arose, which can be seen in sentences such as *I hadn't realised that you already knew my mother*. This meaning has now been borrowed back by the

14

French, so that the French word *realiser* is ambiguous. The meaning 'become aware of' is still considered to be rather vulgar in France, but it is gaining ground. This then is an example of a language that did get its own word back in the end, by borrowing one that had already been borrowed from it.

In most cases, speakers do not object to having their words borrowed. However, in some colonial situations speakers of the colonised language find the term 'borrowing' offensive when their words are taken into the colonising language because it seems to imply co-operation on the part of the lender; in other cases this seems to cause no problem for either party. But despite the problems associated with the term, no alternatives are generally accepted, and we must retain 'borrowing' and 'loan-word'. Some language communities, such as Iceland and France, make positive attempts not to borrow words from outside, this sometimes being seen as demeaning to the borrowing language. Other communities are much more relaxed about this.

Two kinds of borrowing can be distinguished, although the two categories frequently overlap. The first is the kind of borrowing that takes place when the borrowing of the word accompanies the borrowing of the item that it denotes. In these cases the word is almost always borrowed from the language of the area where the item is usually found. Clear examples are provided by words for foods and wildlife that have been borrowed into English.

EXERCISE ✎

3.1 Can you guess where each of the words listed below has been borrowed from?

Words borrowed	Source language
barbecue	
bouillabaisse	
chocolate	
curry	
frankfurter	
molasses	
moussaka	
paella	
smorgasbord	
spaghetti	
tea	
tomato	
coyote	
gnu	
jackal	
jaguar	
kangaroo	

kiwi
macaw
mammoth
merino
orang-utan
springbok

Sometimes people borrow words for reasons of prestige. In these cases it might fairly be claimed that there is no real need for the borrowed word or phrase. In such cases the use of the borrowed word may tell us more about the speaker or writer than about the state of the language. Words and phrases in this category are sometimes (though not always) used consciously to impress or to display learning. These are words like *soupçon* (French) instead of *hint* or *suspicion*, *inter alia* (Latin) instead of *among other things*, *ipso facto* (Latin) instead of *by that very fact*, *ça ne fait rien* (occasionally *san fairy ann* as a representation of the English pronunciation) (French) instead of *it doesn't matter*, *mañana* (Spanish) instead of *it will get done eventually*. In some cases sayings or proverbs are borrowed, as with *che sarà sarà*, *Kinder Kirche Küche*, *liberté égalité fraternité* (respectively, Italian: 'what will be will be'; German: 'children, church, kitchen' (the supposed role of women); and French: 'freedom, equality, brotherhood'). For people who speak the source languages, some of these expressions undoubtedly express cultural values as well as their purely linguistic content, and are thus felt to be more effective than their English translations. This point is not necessarily true for all the people who use these words and phrases, though.

EXERCISE ✎

3.2   What words can you think of borrowed from either French or Italian into English? Do the words borrowed suggest that there are particular areas in which French and Italian have been thought to have particular prestige? If you find such areas, can you think why there should have been such prestige in these areas?

In the history of English, loan-words from four different languages have played a role of particular importance. We will keep coming back to words from these languages throughout the book. First we find words borrowed from the Scandinavian languages (principally Danish) before the Norman conquest in 1066. These words are invisible to all but the expert these days. They include such fundamental words as *she* and *they*, *sister* and *law*, *give* and *take*. In a few cases we have kept both the Scandinavian loan-word and its native English equivalent, now distinguished either in terms of dialects which use them or in terms of meaning. Such pairs of words are often called

Doublets   DOUBLETS. A few examples are given on the next page.

Scandinavian word	Native English equivalent
bairn	child
hale	whole
kirk	church
nay	no
skin	hide
skirt	shirt
sky	heaven

The next, very important, group of loan-words is those that have come from French. Some of these, like *castle*, came into English before the Norman conquest, but many were introduced in the years after the Norman conquest when all the lords and priests spoke French. Not surprisingly, they brought with them words for government and religion, and also for fine food and wealth. English continues to borrow words from French today, but among the loans from this early period are *battle*, *biscuit*, *dinner*, *emerald*, *evidence*, *hermit*, *judge*, *miracle*, *parliament*, *plaintiff*, *prayer*, *realm*, *siege*, *tax*, and literally hundreds of others. There are so many French words in English that it sometimes seems that English must be more closely related to French than to German, but just the opposite is the case, as becomes clear when we look at structures and not just vocabulary.

EXERCISE ✎

3.3   Consider each of the marked words in the passages below. They are all loan-words in origin. Can you guess which ones come from French and which ones come from Scandinavian?

> Parish priests, who were now allowed to *marry*, were to be elected by their congregations unless the living was in the *gift* of a *noble*.
>> (Oakley, Stewart, *The Story of Denmark*
>> (London: Faber & Faber, 1972) p. 101)

> Foreign *artisans* and entrepreneurs were encouraged to settle in Denmark, in particular artisans possessing new *skills*.
>> (*Ibid*, p. 110)

As there are doublets between English and the Scandinavian languages, so too there are a few doublets between English and French, such as *ward(en)/guard(ian)* and *wile/guile*, where the version in *gu-* in each case has come into English through French.

The last sources of loan-words to be discussed here are the classical languages, Greek and Latin. Between them, they give us many of our most formal and learned words, though often disguised as English words by ending in *-ion* or *-ic*, or the like. *Admission* and *deduction*, for instance, are, in origin, Latin words, and so are the much simpler-sounding *admit* and *deduce*.

To demonstrate how pervasive Greek and Latin words are, they have been highlighted in the following passage: Latin words in italics, Greek ones in bold. Words originally from one of these languages, but filtered through French, are underlined.

> *Primitive society practices* its **misogyny** in *terms* of taboo and mana which *evolve* into *explanatory* **myth**. In *historical cultures*, this is *transformed* into **ethical**, then *literary*, and in the *modern* **period**, *scientific rationalizations* for the *sexual* **politic**. **Myth** is, of *course*, a *felicitous* advance in the *level* of *propaganda*, since it so often **bases** its *arguments* on **ethics** or **theories** of *origins*.
>
> (Kate Millett, *Sexual Politics*
> (London: Sphere, 1969) p. 51)

EXERCISE ✎

3.4 *Taboo* and *mana* in the passage from *Sexual Politics* are also loan-words. Can you guess which languages they come from? Since *advance* is also a borrowing from French, what generalisation can you find about which words in this passage are native English?

In Chapter 8 we will return and look at doublets between English, French and the classical languages.

One factor which is sometimes cited as limiting borrowing is the sound structure of the lending language. It is claimed that if the sounds in the source language are not pronounceable by speakers of the borrowing language, then the chances of borrowing are much reduced. In fact this rarely makes a great deal of difference. Consider the two French words *début* and *genre*, both of which are used in English. Standard southern British English contains no vowel like the *é* or the *u* in *début*, and has to make do with making the first syllable sound like *day* and the second rhyme with *view*, neither of which is accurate French. English speakers have great difficulty in producing the distinctively nasal vowels like that represented by the *en* in the spelling of *genre*, and end up saying something that sounds like *on*, even though there is only one segment in French and two in English. Neither do most varieties of English have the same kind of *r*-sound that is used in French. None of this has prevented either of these words from being borrowed. Similar comments would apply to *armadillo* from Spanish, *gnocchi* from Italian and *dachshund* from German.

NEW WORDS FROM ENGLISH 1: COMPOUNDS

4

> In this chapter we look at words that are made up from putting two other words together, and see how these can be extended without limit. We also consider the meanings associated with such words, and look at their structures.

The most common and most flexible way of creating new words in English is to put two old words together to form a new word, a compound. A COMPOUND can be defined, rather loosely, as a lexeme which is made up of two (or more) other lexemes (on lexemes, see Chapter 2). So *blackbird*, *childproof*, *headline*, *typewrite*, *wallpaper* are compounds. By this definition, *girlfriend* is also a compound. But while this is the spelling given by *Collins Concise Dictionary of the English Language* and the 9th edition of the *Concise Oxford Dictionary*, *Webster's Third New International Dictionary* gives the spelling *girl friend*. If we take the spelling seriously, we might be led to conclude that this particular item is one word for the editors of *Collins Concise Dictionary of the English Language* but two for the editors of *Webster's Third New International Dictionary*. This would seem to be an inconsistent conclusion. And what about the editors of the 7th edition of the *Concise Oxford Dictionary* who give the spelling *girl-friend*? Does hyphenation count as one word or two? Since *girl friend*, *girl-friend* and *girlfriend* all behave identically in everything except spelling, it seems more sensible to include them all under the same heading. They will accordingly all be called compound words in what follows, despite the possible intervening space.

Compound

19

EXERCISE ✎

4.1 Mark all the compounds in the text below.

The Web browser wars have heated up again with the release of the platform preview of Internet Explorer 4.0 and the third preview version of Netscape Communicator. . . .[F]eatures include an intelligent web searcher and a new search 'pane' which lets users see search engine results and web pages at the same time.

(The *Australian*, 15 April 1997, Section 3, p. 10)

As you see from exercise 4.1, most compounds in English are nouns, though there are also compound adjectives like *bitter-sweet* or *grass-green* and compound verbs like *charcoal-broil* or *baby-sit*.

One of the most fascinating things about noun compounds is the number of different meaning relationships that can hold between the two parts. Consider, for example, the small sample set out below. In these examples, I assume that any compound with two elements in it has the form AB.

Meaning relationship	**Examples**
A CAUSES B	heat rash, shell shock
A IS CAUSED BY B	flu virus
A IS PREVENTED BY B	tetanus jab
B RESEMBLES A	frogman, hairpin bend
A IS AT PLACE B	ant heap, bookshop
B IS AT TIME A	night worker
B IS MADE OF A	rye bread, soap suds
B IS MADE WITH A	needlework
B IS PART OF A	eardrum, shirtsleeve

Given that such a wide range of meaning relationships exists, it is perhaps surprising that we know to interpret a compound such as *seasickness pill* as 'seasickness is prevented by the pill' rather than as 'seasickness is caused by the pill'. There is nothing in the compound itself to show us which is meant. Moreover, this list of meaning relationships is far from exhaustive. There have been many attempts to provide a full list of the possible meaning relationships in compounds, some of them using very specific definitions of the meaning relationships, others using extremely general ones. The numbers of such meaning relationships suggested range from four to well over a hundred. However, all these attempts have failed. They fail because there are a number of compounds where it is extremely difficult to be precise about the meaning relationship that holds between the two elements. Consider, for example, *domino theory*, *goulash communism*, *milk tooth*, *sex appeal* and *spaghetti western*. What exactly is the relationship between *spaghetti* and *western* in *spaghetti western*? It is certainly possible to provide a gloss along the following lines: 'a western made in a country which is char-acterised by a high consumption of spaghetti'. But this gloss is hardly likely to be a very regular type of meaning relationship (although, of course, the existence of *goulash communism* shows that it may not be unique). The other examples cited show equally ungeneral-isable results.

EXERCISE ✎

4.2 A list of familiar compounds is given below. What meaning relationship holds between the elements in each case? Can you think of another compound which has the same meaning relationship holding between the parts? *Catgut, claw hammer, dog biscuit, doormat, health farm, health food, teaspoon.*

With so many different possible meanings, some of them apparently used for just one compound, it seems much more satisfactory and realistic to say that there is no exhaustive series of relationships which can be listed, but that the relationship has to be worked out from the context in each individual case. Of course, in many instances the relationship between the elements will be known, because the compound is known as a whole. This does not, however, invalidate the general point. This type of approach also explains the fact that it is almost always possible to give an interpretation to a compound made up of any two words whatsoever, even when the combination seems totally unlikely. The interpretation may not seem very likely, but that is a restriction on our experience of what goes on in the world, not a restriction on the words that can be put together to make up compounds.

EXERCISE ✎

4.3 What do you think a *rain-snake* might be? What kind of meaning relationship might hold between the two elements? Is there more than one possibility? If you are a member of a group, compare the answers given by other members. Do you agree that all are possible?

The fact that there are so many possible meaning relationships between the elements in compounds has at least two effects. The first, which has already been mentioned, is that it gives rise to poten-tial ambiguity. For example, *the Edinburgh train* can either mean 'the train to Edinburgh' or 'the train from Edinburgh'. Usually it is clear from the context which is meant, although there could be uncer-tainty in some cases. *An Edinburgh taxi*, though, would usually mean 'a taxi which operates in Edinburgh', rather than 'one going to or coming from Edinburgh'.

The second thing to notice about such vagueness in the specification of meaning is that it saves a lot of space. It is for this reason that compounds of this type are so popular in newspaper headlines. They allow far more material to be packed into something which is set in large type. The following examples of headlines including compounds are all taken from The *UK Mail* of 18–24 June 1996:

Pet lovers hit by world panic in bat rabies scare

Holiday Britons in disease scare

Sex-swop weddings rejected

Training run accident puts paid to brave fitness battle

EXERCISE ✎

4.4 Rephrase the headlines above without using any compounds. Note how economical the compounds are in comparison.

The examples cited above show something else about compounds: they are limitless. In what has been said so far, it has been assumed that most compounds are only made up of two elements. But this is not always so. They can be extended indefinitely. Consider, for instance, the following passage from a Dr. Seuss book:

What do you know about tweetle beetles? Well. . .
    When tweetle beetles fight it's called a tweetle beetle battle.
    And when they battle in a puddle it's a tweetle beetle puddle battle.
    AND when tweetle beetles battle with paddles in a puddle, they call it a tweetle beetle puddle paddle battle.
    AND. . . When beetles battle beetles in a puddle paddle battle and the beetle battle puddle is a puddle in a bottle they call this a tweetle beetle bottle puddle paddle battle muddle. . .
                    (Dr. Seuss, *Fox in Socks* (London: Collins, 1965))

The compound describing the battle gets longer and longer in the course of this passage, and there is no reason why it should not get still longer. In fact, it does in the book, although it also becomes very muddled. One of the interesting things about long compounds such as these is that it is almost always possible to break them down into two elements, each of which can be broken down into two elements, and so on, until the individual words are reached. Consider, for example, *the tweetle beetle puddle paddle battle*. This compound describes a kind of *paddle battle*, so those two elements obviously belong together, and we can link them as in the diagram below. We also know that the creatures that have them are *tweetle beetles*, so those two words are linked. We discover that this is a special kind of *paddle battle*, so we link first *puddle* and then *tweetle beetle* to *paddle battle*. We then have the following analysis:

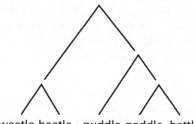

tweetle beetle   puddle paddle battle

Except with a few compounds like *Rank-Hovis-McDougal*, this kind of analysis should work all the time (although there may be cases where it is not absolutely clear how best to analyse a given compound). This means that even the longest compound is made up of two elements, and justifies talking in terms of the two parts of any compound.

EXERCISE ✎

4.5   The following headline occurred in The *Australian* for 15 April 1997: *NZ doubt on <u>Iran exports trade ban</u>*. Draw the tree for the underlined compound.

Since the meaning relationships that hold between the two parts of a compound are not strictly limited, and since there is no limit to the length of compounds, there is nothing to prevent anyone making up their own compounds.

EXERCISE ✎

4.6   On the pattern of the story about tweetle beetles, try to make up your own story with a compound that becomes longer and longer. Can you make a compound that is ten elements long? Does it remain understandable in the context of your story?

People make up their own compounds all the time, as can be seen by looking carefully at any newspaper. Although many of the compounds found in the pages of our newspapers can be found in the larger dictionaries, there are many which cannot. These are created as the need for them arises. Young children also create their own compounds, and from a very early age. It is evidently a process which they find very simple. As long as the first element is the most salient feature of the particular thing they want to talk about, it is hard to go wrong. For example, one two-year-old had a musical box with a picture of a dog on the front of it, and didn't know what to call it. Since it made music, it seemed perfectly obvious to him that it must be some kind of radio. The crucial thing about this one, as opposed to other radios he was familiar with, was that it had a picture of a dog on it. He therefore called it a *dog radio*. The compound is unfamiliar to us, but perfectly understandable in context. This shows that anyone can create new compounds which are perfectly comprehensible: try it for yourself.

FOLLOW-UP READING

The main academic works to be read on the subject of compounds are Valerie Adams, *An Introduction to Modern English Word-Formation* (London: Longman, 1973) and Laurie Bauer, *English Word-Formation* (Cambridge: Cambridge University Press, 1983).

NEW WORDS FROM ENGLISH 2: DERIVATIVES

5

> In this chapter we look at words that are created by adding affixes to already existing words, and discover that some affixes are very selective about what they can be added to.

In the last chapter we saw that we can make new English words by sticking two words together to form a compound. In this chapter we are going to consider how we make new words without starting with two words. We are still interested in sticking two bits together, but here one of the bits is not a word in its own right. Rather it is something which can be found only as a part of other words and which has a very general meaning. These bits are called AFFIXES. The affixes in the words below have been put in bold type, and separated off (where necessary) by a decimal point: *be·head*, *discuss·ion*, *form·al·is·able*, *pre-pay*, *un·familiar·ity*. New words (strictly, new lexemes; see Chapter 2) made with affixes in this manner are called DERIVATIVES.

Affixes

Derivatives

  Only some of the recurrent sequences of letters (or sounds, in the spoken form of the language) which are not words are affixes. Affixes must also have their own meaning (although it may be difficult to specify precisely what that meaning is). For example, the *un-* in *unfamiliarity* means something like 'not', and is also found in other words like *unnatural*, *unlikely*, *uninspiring*, etc. But although there are other words such as *uncle*, *undercoat*, *uniform*, *unit* which begin with the same letters (and in some cases, the same sounds as well), these words do not have the affix *un-* because the bit that is left if the affix is removed is not a word of English and the *un-* does not have the appropriate meaning.

EXERCISE ✎

5.1 Below are several words all of which begin with the letters *dis-*. In some of these, this is an affix. What does the affix mean? In which words is it an affix, and in which words is it not? *Disaster, diskette, disconnect, discontinue, discuss, disengage, disinfect, disorder, displease, distress.*

You cannot just add affixes to words at random. To begin with, there seems to be a limit to the number you can add. The most affixes
Prefixes
you can add before a word (where the affixes are called PREFIXES) seems to be about three; the most you can after a word (where the
Suffixes
affixes are called SUFFIXES) seems to be about five. Even very long and unusual words like *praetertranssubstantiationalistically* only get above the limit of five if you count both *-istic-* and *-ical-* as two affixes (and people disagree about both of these). There may be no reason in principle why you could not write music using *hemidemisemihemidemisemiquavers* (which would be the British expression for what Americans would call '1/512 notes'), but people seem not to, and seem not to need that many prefixes. There may be no reason in principle why you could not have a word like *institutionalisationalisationalise*, but you probably cannot work out what the word would mean, or why it would mean something different from the same word with the last *-ationalise* removed!

EXERCISES ✎

5.2 Think of the longest ordinary English word you know (that is, avoid Welsh or Aboriginal or Native American place names). If you can't think of any, look in your dictionary for a long word. Then see how many prefixes and suffixes you can find in it.

5.3 Start with an adjective that ends in *-al* (perhaps *legal*). Now add *-ise*. What does the word mean? (You might answer 'make legal'.) Then add *-ation*. What does the word mean now? Now go back and add another *-al*. What does the word mean now? How much further can you go? When does it stop making sense to add more affixes?

As you see from exercise 5.3, we can add the affix *-ise* to the affix *-al*, and the affix *-ation* to the affix *-ise*, but we can't add *-ation* directly to *-al*: *legalation* is not a possible word of English. The reason is probably fairly obvious: *-ation* needs to be added to a verb, and *legal* is not a verb, it is an adjective. Some affixes are very selective about what parts of speech they are added to, others are much more flexible. The suffix *-ly* that makes adverbs like *legally, surely,* *abusively* can only be added to adjectives. But the prefix *counter-* can be added to adjectives (*counter-productive*), nouns (*counter-espionage*) or verbs (*counter-sign*) equally well.

Notice that all this talk about adding an affix to a word means that, just as we could draw tree diagrams for compounds (see Chapter 4), so we can draw them for derivatives. And it is usually the case that the trees split in two at each step, just as it was with compounds. As an example, consider *un·fruit·ful·ness*. We start off with the whole word *fruit*. To that, we cannot add *un-* because *unfruit* does not exist; rather, we add *-ful* to give the adjective *fruitful*. Next it appears that we might add either *un-* (*unfruitful*) or *-ness* (*fruitfulness*). We need to think about what the word means. If we add *un-* first to give *unfruitful* and then *-ness*, the whole word will mean 'the quality of being unfruitful', since we are adding *-ness* 'the quality of being' to *unfruitful*; on the other hand, if we add *-ness* first (and then add *un-* to *fruitfulness*) the whole word will mean 'not the quality of being fruitful'. I hope you agree that the first of these is the true meaning of the word, so its structure must be as in the tree below (in which 'A' stands for Adjective and 'N' stands for Noun, and the form under the branches labelled 'A' is an adjective, and so on):

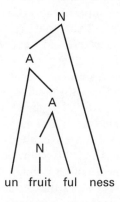

5.4 Draw trees to show the structures of the following words: *disappearance, hopefully, unthinkable.* Can you see a problem with drawing a tree for *undoable*?

5.5 Consider the following words, think about how you would draw the trees, and then see if you can say what kinds of word *un-* can attach to. *Unadventurous, unfairly, unmeasurable, unrhythmically, unsensational, untruthfulness.*

Apart from attaching only to words which belong to the appropriate parts of speech, affixes can be selective about what they will attach to in other ways. For example, there are many different affixes which form nouns from verbs. Consider the pairs *arrive*, *arrival*; *depart*, *departure*; *destroy*, *destruction*; *enlighten*, *enlightenment*; *justify*, *justification*; *laugh*, *laughter*; *marry*, *marriage*; and so on. But if a verb ends in *-ise* you can get only *-isation*. Let's invent a new word. To *lawnise* might mean 'to put a lawn down in or round a place', as in *My grandfather's just lawnised his new house*, but you've never heard the word before. But you know that you will have to talk about the *lawnisation* of your grandfather's house, and not the *lawnisal*, the *lawnisure*, the *lawnision*, the *lawnister* and so on. There is only one possibility. Similarly, there is only one possibility for making nouns out of verbs that end in the affixes *-ate* or *-ify*.

EXERCISE ✎

5.6   What are the patterns for verbs that end in *-ate* and *-ify*? Find an example of each.

Although there are many other restrictions on what affixes can go on what words, perhaps the most important of these depends on etymology, that is on the source of the words. Some affixes can attach only to words (or to other affixes) that are derived from Latin; some can attach only to words (or other affixes) which are native English; some are not selective. For instance, *-ity* will only attach to Latinate words, such as *generous*, *legal* or *portable*. Note that it attaches to *washable* to give *washability*. But *wash* is a native English word: it has cognates (see Chapter 10) in languages like German and Danish. The Latinate quality must be in the suffix *-able*. The suffix *-able*, itself, is one which is not selective about whether it attaches to Latinate or native words. The suffix *-en* which makes adjectives from nouns such as *waxen*, on the other hand, resists Latinate bases, and attaches only to native ones, so that although *golden*, *waxen* and *wooden* are perfectly ordinary, we cannot find words such as *manganesen*, *resinen* or *sycamoren*.

Generally speaking, users of English manage all these restrictions unconsciously, and make up new words as they need them. But they cannot make up new words with any old affix, even if they stick to the right parts of speech and the right rules for Latinateness and so on. For instance, you may have heard of *oaken* chests. But if you were given an chest made of elmwood, could you thank the giver for the *elmen* chest? What if the chest was made of larch, pine or plane? Not even *ashen* is acceptable, although *ashen* is an English word meaning 'having the colour of ashes' rather than 'made from ash wood'. It seems we cannot use this affix at all to make new words, though we recognise it in old ones. We say this affix is not PRODUCTIVE. We have already seen, though, that we can make up new words with *-ise*, so this affix is productive. Different affixes have been productive at different periods of history, and have left traces

Productive

behind them in the form of words we still use. But while it is always difficult to say that a particular affix will never be used again, many familiar ones are not used or are very infrequently used in the creation of new words. Productivity ensures that not every new word which looks possible is actually possible.

EXERCISE ✎

5.7   Consider the following brief quotation:

> He died. You want the technical explanation or you want it in laymanese?
>
> (Thomas, Ross, *The Mordida Man*
> (London: Hamish Hamilton, 1981), p. 19)

You have probably never heard the word *laymanese* before; it is not listed in any of the dictionaries I have consulted. What does this suggest? Could you use the suffix *-ese* to create new words? Does the knowledge that *phoneticianese*, *policese* and *spookese* (*spook* meaning 'spy') are also attested in print make any difference to your conclusion?

6 MEANING RELATIONSHIPS

In this chapter we consider the ways in which words can be related to each other in terms of their meaning.

This chapter and the next one form a pair which look at words from two complementary sides. In this chapter we will consider the ways in which words are related in terms of their meanings; in the next we will consider how they are related in terms of their form.

Perhaps the most obvious meaning relationship between two words is that they can both mean the same thing. In this case, we

Synonyms

talk of the two words being SYNONYMS. When we say that what Americans call a *truck* the British call a *lorry*, we are saying that *truck* and *lorry* are synonyms. Near-synonyms are exploited in dictionary definitions (e.g. **fray** 'to wear (as an edge of cloth)' in *Merriam Webster's Collegiate Dictionary*). If we take synonyms to be words which always mean the same thing so that one of them can replace the other in absolutely any sentence, then synonyms are extraordinarily rare. Usually synonyms differ in that they are used in different dialects, in different styles, in different combinations or in that the meanings of two words may overlap, but each has its own area as well. For instance, *freedom* and *liberty* are commonly treated as synonyms (and either could be used of someone who had just come out of captivity in the sentence *She is enjoying her freedom/ liberty*), but they appear in different combinations, because although we have *freedom of expression* and *academic freedom* there is no general corresponding *liberty of expression* or *academic liberty*. Equally, the meaning of *liberty* is not fully contained within the meaning of *freedom*, because the meaning in *She took a real liberty!* is peculiar to *liberty*, and not available for *freedom*. You will find the term synonym used in two slightly different ways: either it is used to say that two words have the same meaning in some particular context, or it is used in a wider sense to mean that two lexemes always have precisely the same meaning. Here, I shall use the second of these; in most cases very little hinges on which is meant.

EXERCISE ✎

6.1 Find places in which *pail* and *bucket* cannot be used to replace each other despite their closeness of meaning, and ways in which *torch* and *flash-light* are not true synonyms.

If synonyms in this wider sense are rare, there are large numbers of antonyms, or words that are opposite in meaning. The term antonym is used rather loosely in ordinary language to talk about the way in which *buy* is 'opposite to' *sell*, *husband* is 'opposite to' *wife* and *good* is 'opposite to' *bad*, even though these are rather different kinds of 'opposite'. Linguists prefer to restrict the term ANTONYM to those **Antonym** opposites which are labelled by adjectives as being at the opposite ends of some scale, and which can thus be seen as being GRADABLE: **Gradable** *good* versus *bad*, *deep* versus *shallow*, *pleased* versus *displeased* and *desirable* versus *undesirable*.

EXERCISE ✎

6.2 Which of the following words has a gradable antonym, and what is it? *Big, borrow, dead, polite, son.*

William Brown in the *Just William* books by Richmal Crompton says on one occasion that the opposite of *dog* is *cat*. This is a very different kind of 'opposite' from the gradable antonym kind of opposite. Let us say that words like *dog* and *cat* are INCOMPATIBLE **Incompatible** – nothing can be a *dog* and a *cat* at the same time. There are several different types of incompatibility. The one we have with the case of *dog* and *cat* can be discussed under the label of HYPONYMY. **Hyponymy**

Dogs and cats are both kinds of animal. If it is true that we can say that *every dog is an animal, a dog is a kind of animal, I saw some dogs and other animals*, then we can say that *dog* is a HYPONYM **Hyponym** of *animal* and that *animal* is a SUPERORDINATE of *dog*. If we try the **Superordinate** same exercise with *cat*, we find that *cat* is also a hyponym of *animal*, and that *animal* is a superordinate term for *cat*. *Dog* and *cat* are CO- **Co-hyponym** HYPONYMS of the superordinate term *animal*. We could find a number of other hyponyms of *animal*, such as *elephant*, *frog* and *goat*. We could also find some words which are hyponyms of *dog* and *cat*, for example *bitch, puppy, Rottweiler; tom, kitten*, and so on. So we can find hierarchies of hyponymy.

Although *dog* is a superordinate of *bitch*, as we have seen, there is another sense in which *dog* is incompatible with *bitch*: in this sense *dog* means specifically 'male dog'. We have to decide at this point

Polysemous

whether there are two different lexemes (say DOG¹ and DOG²) or whether DOG is a POLYSEMOUS lexeme (one with more than one meaning). Both usages are found. In either case, we can draw a diagram as follows, where superordinate terms are higher up the page than their hyponyms, each of which is linked to its superordinate by a branch; co-hyponyms are on the same level and share a superordinate:

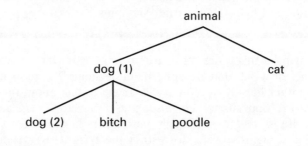

EXERCISES ✎

6.3 Which of the following words are hyponyms of *animal*? *Ant, bear, octopus, robin, snail, sponge, tiger, whale.*

6.4 Which of the following words are hyponyms of others on the list? Draw a diagram to show the relationships between the words. *Daffodil, dandelion, elm, flower, honeysuckle, oak, object, plant, rose, weed, yew.*

Co-hyponyms between them build up networks of meaning, in which the limits of the meanings of the individual words are constrained and defined by the meanings of the other words in the network. The most obvious case of this type is colour terminology. Every language has words for colour, but not every language has the same number of such words, and not every language divides up the spectrum in the same way. One celebrated example of this is the different ways in which English and Welsh – at least rather old-fashioned Welsh – divide up parts of the colour spectrum:

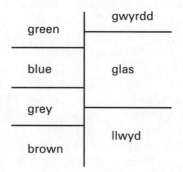

Although this particular example has been often cited by linguists, such examples could be given from a number of different language pairs. Tiv, a language of Nigeria, has only three basic colour terms, while Hungarian has twelve, so clearly the colour terms in these two languages do not match precisely. The important thing to notice about this particular example, though, is that the meaning of *blue* is best given as being 'a colour which lies between *green* and *grey*', just as the meaning of Welsh *glas* is 'a colour which lies between *gwyrdd* and *llwyd*'. Their meaning is determined by the other terms in the system.

EXERCISE ✎

6.5 Find a range of colour terms. Which ones are hyponyms of which? Which ones are best defined in terms of which other ones?

Although the colour terms provide a particularly clear example, words which come from the same LEXICAL FIELD in this way can always be seen as being defined in terms of their co-hyponyms. And just as different languages divide up the colour spectrum differently, so different languages can divide up other lexical fields in different ways. A notorious example is provided by words for snow in Eskimo. Eskimo is frequently said to divide the lexical field of snow up far more finely than English does, for the simple reason that the different kinds of snow are culturally far more important to speakers of Eskimo languages than they are to speakers of English. There are all kinds of problems with this general statement. If you know that estimates of the number of Eskimo snow words vary from two to about fifty, you will immediately suspect that the story has not suffered in the retelling. And as you might suspect (given what was said in Chapter 2) part of the difficulty seems to be what kinds of 'word' you count (word-forms or lexemes? do compounds count as new words or not?). The story is a good one because we feel it ought to be true that things have more words for them the more cultur-ally important they are. On that basis, drunkenness must be very culturally important in English, since English thesauruses list some fifty words for being drunk.

Lexical field

EXERCISE ✎

6.6 How many English words can you find for snow or ice in different forms? One Eskimo language has different words (different lexemes) for at least the following: snow which is falling, wet snow which is falling, new-fallen snow, rotten snow on the sea, wet snow on the ground; there are also words for ice in different conditions. Can you match these from English? Do you think it is true that English and Eskimo divide up the lexical field of snow words differently?

Besides being determined by co-hyponyms, the meaning of a word is also determined by the other words it occurs with. Consider the word *dry*. *Dry* means something different when we talk about *dry wine* from what it means when we talk about *dry clothes*. When we talk about a *dry wit* or a *dry-stone wall* it has other meanings again. In fact, it is hard to give a meaning for the word *dry* unless we know what company it has been found in, that is what COLLOCATIONS it occurs in.

Collocation

Some words occur in very restricted collocations. The word *blonde*, for instance, collocates with *hair* and its hyponyms (*wig, moustache, plait,* etc.) or with *wood* and its hyponyms (*oak,* etc.). The word *kith* is so restricted in its collocations that it only ever occurs in the phrase *kith and kin.*

EXERCISE ✎

6.7 What nouns can *hard* collocate with? What adjectives and verbs can the noun *ground* collocate with? How do these collocations reflect meaning?

Not only words, but affixes can have restricted collocations in this way. We have seen in Chapter 5 that some affixes are very selective in the bases they occur with, but some are so selective that they only ever occur with one or two. The suffix *-ter* that occurs in *laughter* may only occur with one other word, the word *slaughter* (and you may not think it even occurs there). The word *bishopric* contains a suffix *-ric* which occurs only when attached to the word *bishop*. In ways like this, affixes behave very much like words do. Affixes may also show synonymy; for instance: *-ness* and *-ity* in *productiveness* and *productivity* mean virtually the same, but tend to be used in different contexts (*-ity* being preferred in more technical contexts).

Despite these similarities, however, affixes also show differences from ordinary words in their meanings. While the meaning of an affix such as the *-ling* in *duck·ling* seems to be very similar to the meanings of words like *little* or *young*, the meaning of an affix like *-er* in *walk·er* is much vaguer. We might want to translate it as 'person who carries out the action of the verb in a habitual way'; we might summarise this as 'actor' or 'agent' or something similar, and in particular we might want to draw the parallel between the action of walking and the actor who is the walker. When we get down to the affixes in words like *transport·ation*, the meaning of the affix is getting very difficult to specify. And the meaning of the suffix in *parent·al* might be no more than 'this word is an adjective'. In short, affixes seem to show a range of types of meaning from the specific, lexical meanings we associate with words to very general grammatical meanings.

EXERCISE ✎

6.8 What do you think the meaning of the suffix is in each of the following words? *Cheap·ness*, *dish-wash·er*, *pay·ee*, *photograph·ic*, *visual·ise*.

FOLLOW-UP READING

For examples of synonyms and antonyms, see any thesaurus. For collocations see many dictionaries, but in particular Morton Benson, Evelyn Benson and Robert Ilson, *The BBI Combinatory Dictionary of English* (Amsterdam and Philadelphia: Benjamins, 1986). The example of Welsh colour terms comes from Louis Hjelmslev, *Omkring Sprogteoriens Grundlæggelse* (Copenhagen: Akademisk, 1943), p. 49. My information on Eskimo snow words is taken from Michael Fortescue, *West Greenlandic* (London, etc.: Croom Helm, 1984), pp. 366–367.

7 FORMAL RELATIONSHIPS

> In this chapter we consider the ways in which words can be related to each other in terms of their form – their sound or their spelling.

In the last chapter we looked at the ways in which the meanings of words provide links between them. In this chapter we move on to consider the formal links between words, links of sound or spelling, and sometimes other more abstract links.

If the most obvious meaning relationship between words is synonymy, the most obvious formal relationship between words is identity of form. While we saw that real synonymy is rare, identity of form is common. We can look at identity of form in the sound **Homophone** of the word, when we talk about the words being HOMOPHONES, or identity of form in the spelling of the word, in which case we talk **Homograph** of the words being HOMOGRAPHS. For example, you will almost certainly at some stage in your school career have made a mistake in writing *there* for *their* or vice versa. Although these two words are written differently, they sound precisely the same. They are homophones. On the other hand, the form *read* is pronounced differently in the sentences *I want you to read this poem for tomorrow* and *He read the entire book in under two hours*. *Read* represents two words here, and these words are homographs. Many words are both homographs and homophones. For example, the words written *shed* in *The snake has shed its skin* and *I put the spade in the shed* are written and pronounced identically, although they belong to separate lexemes. Words which are both homophones and homo- **Homonym** graphs are sometimes referred to as HOMONYMS.

36

7.1 How do you know that there are two distinct words *shed* if they are written and pronounced the same way?

7.2 Can you find a word which is either a homograph or a homophone or both for each of the following words? *Polish, bear, common, cuff, supply, two*.

Sometimes the kind of English you speak determines whether or not two words are homophones, though the fairly standardised spelling of English does not allow much room for words to be homographs in only a few varieties. For example, some Scots and New Zealanders pronounce *pull* and *pool* identically; speakers from the south-east of England and Australia, but not from America, pronounce *father* and *farther* identically; some Scots and Canadians distinguish between *tide* and *tied*; and so on.

Homophones are widely used in the construction of puns and other jokes. For example, the junior-school verse of 'Mary Had a Little Lamb' reproduced below plays obviously on the homophony of *bear* and *bare* and less obviously on the homonymy of two words *her* (if you replace *Mary* with *Henry*, the joke will not work).

> Mary had a little lamb
> She also had a bear.
> I've often seen her little lamb
> But never seen her bear.

7.3 Think of some more jokes that depend on homophony to work.

As well as having whole words which have identical form, we find bits of words which have identical form. Sometimes these bits of identical form are purely coincidental and do not obviously affect our perception of the words concerned. For instance, we should not usually notice that *entry* and *mutton* both contain an [n] sound. This is just the result of the fact that we have a lot of words and a relatively small number of possible sounds, and that we have to use the sounds over and over again.

It is part of the way that language works that there is – on the whole – no direct relationship between the form of a word and its meaning. Although we often feel that there is an essential rightness to the name of some object, a little thought will make it clear that this cannot be the case. There is a story of a farmer looking over the wall of the pigsty at his animals and saying 'Rightly are they called pigs!' An equivalent story is the one about the child who is

Onomatopoeia

supposed to have said 'They're called pigs because they're such swine.' But although we may feel that *pig* is a good name for that particular animal, Danes feel the same way about the word *gris*, Frenchman the same about the word *cochon*, Germans the same about the word *Schwein*, and Xhosa speakers the same about *ihagu*. All speakers feel that the word for 'pig' in their language is an appropriate one, even though they have little or nothing in common in terms of their sounds or spelling. There are, of course, exceptions – but only relative ones. There are some words whose sound does represent their meaning: words like *bow-wow* for the noise made by a dog. This phenomenon of using sounds to represent the meaning is called ONOMATOPOEIA, and has a special name because it is so rare. But although we think that *bow-wow* captures the sound of a dog barking, we need to recall that Danish dogs say *vov-vov*, French dogs say *ouâ-ouâ*, and Russian ones say *gav-gav*. Even these onomatopoeic words are filtered through linguistic and cultural perceptions.

EXERCISE ✎

7.4 Below is a list of Japanese words for animal noises. What animal do you think makes each noise? Note that if you cannot tell immediately, it implies that the word is not a direct representation of the sound, even though Japanese speakers would see each as being onomatopoeic. Also, if you do not know what animals make these noises, it implies that a Japanese speaker would have the same difficulty with the English words. *Bū-bū*, *chū-chū*, *gā-gā*, *hi-hi-in*, *mē-mē*, *mō-mō*, *nyā-nyā*, *wan-wan*.

Alliteration
Rhyme

The phenomena of ALLITERATION and RHYME make the most of random similarities of sound between words to draw attention to the words. W. S. Gilbert was a master of both, as can be seen from the following brief examples:

> Awaiting the sensation of a short, sharp shock,
> From a cheap and chippy chopper on a big black block.
> (From *The Mikado*)

> Then a sentimental passion of a vegetable fashion must excite your languid spleen,
> An attachment à la Plato for a bashful young potato, or a not too French French bean!
> (From *Patience*)

But the similarity in form between *cheap* and *chopper* does not carry any meaning with it. There are cases, though, where a particular form does appear to be associated with some meaning (perhaps rather vaguely specified meaning) in a number of words. Consider, for example, the words *sleazy, sleet, slick, slide, slime, slink, slip, slippery*, *slither*, *slug*, *slurry* and *slush*. All of these seem to have something to do with something unpleasant involving slipperiness and moisture. We say that there is a PHONAESTHEME, [sl], with some such meaning appearing in these words.

Phonaestheme

Notice that the consonant cluster [sl] does not necessarily always have the same connotations. There are words beginning in [sl] which might seem pleasant words, dealing neither in slipperiness or moisture.

EXERCISES ✎

7.5 Which of the following words do you think contain the same phonaestheme as that in the words given above? If you are a member of a group, do all the members of the group agree? *Slander*, *slang*, *slant*, *slash*, *slate*, *slave*, *slay*, *sledge*, *sleep*, *sleuth*, *slice*, *slob*, *slope*, *slovenly* and *slow*.

7.6 Which of the following sets of words do you think contains a phonaestheme? If you think there is one, approximately what do you think its meaning is? Do all the listed words share the phonaestheme? Can you find other words with similar sequences of letters/sounds which do not have the same connotations?

(a) *glamour*, *glance*, *glare*, *glass*, *glaze*, *glimmer*, *glimpse*, *glint*, *glitter*, *gloss*, *glow*.
(b) *bump*, *clump*, *jump*, *lump*, *thump*.
(c) *fraction*, *fragile*, *frail*, *frame*, *frantic*, *fraud*, *freckle*, *free*, *freeze*, *fresh*, *fret*, *fringe*, *front*, *frost*.

In very special instances, we find those places where a particular bit of sound-form or a sequence of letters is firmly associated with a particular meaning and where the whole word is exhaustively analysable into these chunks. Some of these chunks will be the affixes we met in Chapter 5. Some of them will be words in their own right. When we want to refer to all of these together, independent of their status as words or affixes, we call them MORPHEMES. A word like *uncountable* contains the morphemes {un}, {count} and {able} (these are written within braces to show we are discussing them as morphemes). The trees that we drew in Chapter 5 were trees of the morphemes that make up longer words.

Morpheme

EXERCISE ✎

7.7 What are the morphemes in each of the following words? Find another word in which each morpheme appears. *Predetermined*, *pressures*, *undulates*, *unfriendly*.

When we put morphemes together into words, we sometimes find changes taking place in the forms of those morphemes. Sometimes our spelling shows those changes, and sometimes it does not.

Consider the prefix *in-* meaning 'not' in words like *inactive, indecent, inorganic* and so on. What happens to that morpheme if we put it in front of a word beginning with a *p* or an *m*? Possible words include *probable, possible, mature* and *mobile*. Instead of writing or saying *in·probable, in·mature* and so on, we write and say *im·probable, im·possible, im·mature* and *im·mobile*. The morpheme {in} takes on the form *im-* when it is followed by a *p* or an *m*, because the sounds [p] and [m] are both made with the lips closed.

But consider the words *cats* and *dogs*. Each of these contains the plural morpheme {s}, which we write in both cases with the letter *s*. Yet they are not pronounced the same way. At the end of *cats* we find a [s] sound, like the one at the beginning of *sip*, while at the end of *dogs* we find a [z] sound, like the one at the beginning of *zip*. If you try to say *cats* with a [z] at the end or *dogs* with a [s], you will probably find it very difficult indeed. But in this case our spelling does not show the difference.

Morphophonemics

Change in the phonetic shapes of morphemes depending on the words they occur in is called MORPHOPHONEMICS.

EXERCISES ✎

7.8 What happens to the morpheme {in} which was discussed above when it is added to words beginning with the sounds [l] and [r]? Distinguish what happens in sound from what happens in spelling. Give examples.

7.9 Consider the following pairs of words: *sign, signature; malign, malignant; phlegm, phlegmatic*. What morphophonemic changes can you observe in these words? Why isn't *sign* spelled *sine* in English, to match its pronunciation?

There are places where there are morphographemic changes in words which do not reflect any change in sound. For instance, consider the word *friendly*. If we add the suffix *-ness*, we have to change the spelling of *friendly* to *friendli*, to give *friendliness*. The sounds of *friendly* have not changed, only the spelling. This is the converse of those instances – like the one illustrated in exercise 7.9 – where the spelling does not change, but the sound does. If we were writing the morphemes in the word *friendliness*, we would say that they are {friend}, {ly} and {ness}.

STYLISH WORDS

8

> This chapter deals with the relationship between words and style, showing how some kinds of words are found in particular contexts, and how the kinds of words that are used can vary with formality and technicality.

Imagine yourself talking to a small baby boy who is too young to talk back. You might say something like: 'Who's a clever little chappie, then? Are you going to give me a smile? A nice B-I-G smile for me? What a clever baby!' You might manage to say something more sensible, but most people don't. There are certain facets of this monologue which show that it is directed at a baby. The use of a lot of questions (usually with exaggerated intonation patterns), for instance. But some of the features that show how the language is being used are to do with vocabulary. Words like *nice*, *little* and *big* for instance, might be perfectly normal in all kinds of conversations, but tend to get overused in language to small children. The use of the diminutive form *chappie* is not restricted to language addressed to children, but diminutives tend to get used far more often in this context than in others. It would be ridiculous if a chemistry teacher at a secondary school used the same kind of language in a class, and said 'Well, we'll take a nice little beaker, won't we, and heat it up on a tripod-ie. Aren't we clever students?' The way we talk and the words we use change depending on the context we use them in. In the sense that the choice of words varies with context and audience we can talk of them as being linked to STYLE.   **Style**

In a book called *Vocabulary*, we are naturally concentrating on the way in which different words are used in different styles; but different grammatical constructions are also used in different styles, and may be just as important for distinguishing between formal and informal language. If you are thinking about style in general, you

41

should consider grammatical patterns just as much as the vocabulary which is the focus of attention here.

EXERCISE ✎

8.1 Consider the poem below, whose translation into normal English should be familiar to you. How much of the effect of this poem is due to the words chosen, how much to the grammatical constructions used? Try writing an equivalent version of 'This is the House that Jack Built'.

> Scintillate, scintillate, aster vivific.
> Fain would I fathom thy nature specific.
> Freely suspended in ether capacious,
> Strongly resembling a gem carbonaceous.

In most contexts, much of the choice of vocabulary is dependent upon the subject matter to be discussed. For instance, the moment you start talking about cricket you will need to use words such as *bat*, *wicket*, *ball*, *stumps*, *wicket-keeper* and *silly mid on*. This kind of vocabulary is called JARGON, and there is a jargon for almost every subject, although you may not know the jargon for television engineering or open-heart surgery. One of the reasons that it is impossible to give a full list of all the words of English is that there are jargons for so many areas: nobody can know all the jargons.

Jargon

EXERCISE ✎

8.2 What subject are the following sets of jargon words associated with?

    (a) *goal, winger, centre-forward, back, header, free kick.*
    (b) *prefix, productive, compound, suffix, Latinate.*
    (c) *joy-stick, aileron, rudder, flaps, undercarriage.*
    (d) *compound, salt, element, molecule, reagent.*
    (e) *tutu, jetée, points, barre, pirouette.*

There are also words which you use to prove that you belong to a particular in-group. Sometimes these words are used to keep things secret from outsiders, like thieves' cant, or the words of Polari (a vocabulary, much of which is based on Italian) which are used in parts of the theatrical profession: words such as *bona* for 'good', *lallies* for 'legs' and *varder* for 'see'. More often, these words just say something about the social group which you belong to. In this sense they are rather like dialect words, except that the group is not defined in regional terms but in social or other terms.

Slang

One example of this is teenage SLANG. You will have words for things which you approve of (*neat, awesome, cool, fab, . . .*), things you disapprove of (*grotty*, *the pits*, *lousy*, *pathetic*, . . .), people you think are stupid (*dick*, *dork*, *drongo*, *nong*, . . .), and it is a fairly sure bet that they will not be the same words your parents used when they were your age. In fact, you may use different words from your siblings, because you use these words to define your group, and the group is often made up of people of the same age.

EXERCISE ✎

8.3 Make a list of the words you use to show your approval of something. Make a list of other words you know which mean the same thing, but which you would not use. Who would use them? What would your reaction be if your parents used the terms that your schoolfriends use?

Another well-known example of this kind of language is Cockney rhyming slang. In Cockney rhyming slang, a particular word is replaced by a phrase which rhymes with the word. Frequently, however, only the first (non-rhyming) part of the phrase is actually used, not the entire phrase. So a *hat* may be called a *tit for*, short for *tit for tat*. Some bits of rhyming slang have become so well-established that they have spread out into more general English, and people are not necessarily aware of where the expressions come from. For instance, *let's have a butcher's* is short for *let's have a butcher's hook*, which rhymes with *look*. *Use your loaf* is short for *use your loaf of bread*, which rhymes with *head*. *To be on your Tod* is short for *to be on your Tod Sloan*, which rhymes with *own*. *That's a load of old cobbler's* is short for *that's a load of old cobbler's awls*, which rhymes with *balls*. *To blow a raspberry* is short for *to blow a raspberry tart*, which rhymes with *fart*.

There are also many bits of Cockney rhyming slang which have become quite well known, but which are still recognised for what they are. Some of these are in the short form (e.g. *Bristols*, short for *Bristol cities*, meaning *titties*, *china*, short for *china plate*, meaning *mate*), others in the long form (e.g. *trouble and strife* for *wife* or *north and south* for *mouth*). All these expressions give the impression that there is a well-established set of rhyming phrases which are used with fixed meanings. To a certain extent this is true, and collections of rhyming slang will give many standard expressions such as *frog and toad* for *road* or *Adam and Eve* for *believe*. But true Cockney rhyming slang also has an impromptu element, where the listener has to guess what the real meaning is from the context, and frequently only with the non-rhyming part of the phrase for a clue.

EXERCISE ✎

8.4 The following passage, liberally sprinkled with bits of rhyming slang, may be hard to interpret. Try to work out what the whole phrase must be as well as the meaning.

I got up this morning, brushed my 'Amsteads and my
Barnet, kissed the dustbin lids and put on my tit for to
go for a ball up the frog. I didn't have much bees, but I
still put an Oxford on a Charing Cross that came in at 20
to 1. I could hardly Adam my Donald! So I went to the
rub-a-dub and had a pig's with some chinas. Only one,
though, because I didn't want to be elephant's when I got
home to the trouble.

On a more general level, English has a built-in measure of style in
the words it uses. On the most everyday level are native English
words. At a slightly higher level, especially if they contrast with
native words, are words borrowed from French. Such words may be
more formal or more literary than the native English words. On a
higher level still are words borrowed from Latin. These may be academic words, technical words, or very formal words. And the words
from the highest level are those whose origins are in Greek. These
are nearly always technical words. As a general rule, the greater the
number of Latin or Greek words there are in a passage, the more
formal or technical that passage will be. We have already seen how
Latin and Greek words can proliferate in formal and technical
writing in Chapter 3, in a passage from Kate Millett's *Sexual Politics*.
A few examples where there are near synonyms or closely related
words derived from different languages will help to make the point.

Native	French origin	Latin origin	Greek origin
tit for tat	revenge	retaliation	
snake	serpent		herpetology
coming	approach	advent	
shift	movement	momentum	kinetics
shiny	brilliant	luminescent	photogenic

Phrasal verb

A special case of this is the distinction between PHRASAL VERBS
(made up of a simple verb and a particle) and verbs of French or
Latin origin. For instance the difference between *Remove your
outdoor clothing* and *Take off your outdoor clothing* is a difference
between a single formal verb and a less formal phrasal verb.

EXERCISE ✎

8.5 Can you find a phrasal verb corresponding to each of the
following verbs? *Alight, ascend, depart, incarcerate, reprove.*

In general, the native words are the ones we learn early and use in
everyday conversation, while the Latin and Greek words are ones
we learn during secondary and tertiary education, or which we use
in technical spheres. Despite this, it can be quite difficult to avoid
all French, Latin and Greek words completely.

EXERCISE ✎

8.6 The following passage mixes native, <u>French</u>, **Latin** and Greek words freely. Rewrite the passage using consistently (a) words which are on the lowest possible style level and (b) words which are on the highest and most technical possible style level. You will probably find that you need to use a thesaurus to do this exercise. What kinds of audience does the passage become suitable for?

On Io, the **gravitational** <u>influence</u> of the three nearby moons is enough to **distort** the shape of the world itself, <u>causing</u> it to <u>pulse</u> with a heartbeat-like *lub-dub*. This RHYTHMIC **motion** churns up **internal** heat, which in turn stirs up moonwide **volcanoes**. Though such otherworldly **erupting** is DRAMATIC, it <u>amounts</u> to little more than GEOLOGICAL PYROTECHNICS.

(*Time*, 21 April 1997, p. 54)

9 TECHNICAL WORDS

In this chapter we look at some of the technical words that are based on Greek and Latin, consider how to work out what they mean and how they are formed.

How much Greek do you speak? None? What about *tyrannosaurus*, *pterodactyl*, *photogenic*, *telekinesis*, *hydrogen*, *geology* and *photograph*? Are all of these words 'Greek to you'? Clearly these are not words of classical Greek. Aristophanes or Plato would have been puzzled as to what they could refer to. Photographs and telephones, mammograms and dinosaurs were not known in classical times. But the words are made up of elements of classical Greek, in the same way that *flittermouse* and *floodtide* are made up of English elements. These technical words based on Greek are words which we tend to meet in the course of our formal education (secondary and tertiary, especially), and ability to cope with formal education can be influenced by ability to work out the meanings of such words. We have already met many words whose origins are Greek in this book, and in this chapter clues will be given to start you on the process of working out what their meanings are likely to be.

We are so used to the word *telephone* meaning the instrument on which we talk to our friends all evening or which beeps in the pockets of yuppies at concerts and plays that we never have to stop and think about why it should mean what it does. But if we split it up into its elements, and find other words which have the same elements, we can see that there is a constant meaning associated with each, whether or not we analyse it when we hear the word (we probably do not analyse *hedgehog* when we hear the word, either; but its elements still have independent meaning). These elements are morphemes (see Chapter 7), though morphemes of a type we have not discussed before.

9.1 The word *telephone* can be split into two meaningful elements *tele-* and *-phone*. Can you find five other words containing the *tele-* element and five other words containing the *-phone* element?

9.2 What meaning do the words containing *tele-* share? What meaning do the words containing *-phon(e)* share?

The words containing *tele-* all have the idea of something happening at a distance. For instance, a *telescope* allows you to see distant objects; *telepathy* allows you to communicate at a distance, without any physical link; and so on. The words containing *-phon(e)* all have something to do with sound. In some cases there is an instrument which transmits sound in some way (*gramophone, hydrophone, megaphone*), in others the connection with sound does not involve an instrument (*phonetics* is the study of speech sounds, for example), but in every case there is a link with sound. A *telephone*, therefore is a 'distance-sound', or something which allows you to hear sound (specifically speech) at a distance. (This can be compared with German *Fernsprecher*, which literally means 'distant speaker', although Germans also use the word *Telephon*. The general idea is much the same.)

   Telephone is typical of this class of words: finding out what the individual elements mean will give you some idea of what the word as a whole is about, but will not be sufficient to pin the word down exactly. Recall that we saw that precisely the same was true of English compounds (see Chapter 3). From 'distance-sound' you have to take that extra leap to find out what a telephone actually is, but you have some idea from the meanings of the individual elements.

9.3 What do you suppose a *geophone* is? You know the *geo-* element from words like *geography, geology, geophysics*, etc.

9.4 Find five words which contain each of the following elements. What does each mean? *Phot(o)-, hydr(o)-, -(o)logy, psych(o)-.*

Why do the elements listed in 9.4 all have a parenthesised *-o-* attached to them? What does the *-o-* do? Words using elements like this, which are called NEO-CLASSICAL COMPOUNDS because they are like compounds, but made from elements of the classical languages (usually Greek), are made up of two Greek words put together in a compound. But in Greek – and this is very different from the

Neo-classical compound

normal state of affairs in English – the basic part of the word cannot stand alone: it needs an ending. The 'ending' which is used in the middle of a compound is nearly always (but not absolutely always, remember *telephone*) the *-o-* that we see in *hydr·o·logy*, for example.

This linking *-o-* may not persist next to a vowel or an *h*. Consider the following words, all listed in the *Oxford English Dictionary*, formed with the element *pseud(o)-* 'false':

Word	Meaning
pseud·andry	the use of a male pseudonym by a female
pseud·haemal	a fluid like blood in some invertebrates
pseud·helminth	something which resembles an entoparasitic worm
pseud·o·branchia	false gills
pseud·o·chromia	false perception of colour
pseud·odont	having horny epidermic teeth
pseud·o·faeces	waste product from molluscs, which has never been through the gut
pseud·osmia	false perception of smell

Not all Greek elements are found without the linking *-o-* in these circumstances (consider *micro-organism*, for instance), but there are sufficient cases for you to expect this pattern of variation.

EXERCISE ✎

9.5 Given a Greek base *leuc* meaning 'white' and other bases *dendron* meaning 'tree', *haemia* meaning 'blood' and the form *anthous* meaning 'having flowers', what would you predict to be the forms for a white tree, white blood and white-flowered?

One set of words made up of classical elements is those technical words ending in *-phobia* which denote fears of particular things. For example, *agoraphobia* is a fear of or aversion to open spaces, *xenophobia* is fear of or aversion to foreigners, and *hydrophobia*, 'rabies', is so-called because one of the symptoms is an aversion to water. Although the meanings of many such words cannot be deduced without a knowledge of the classical languages (usually Greek), in some cases you can work out what they must mean because of other words in English which use the same root. For example, faced with *hydrophobia*, we can look for other words containing the element *hydr(o)-* to see what it might mean. We have seen some of these in response to exercise 9.4. If we know the meanings of these (or other similar words) we can deduce that *hydr(o)-* must have something to do with water, and hence deduce the meaning of *hydrophobia*.

EXERCISE ✎

9.6 Can you deduce the meanings of any of the following words? *Aquaphobia, brontophobia, gymnophobia, logophobia, necrophobia.*

It should be clear to you that the more such words you know, the easier it becomes to understand others.

10 WHERE WORDS COME FROM: ETYMOLOGY

> This chapter is concerned with the origins of words and finding relationships between words based on their history. The concern here is to point out how scientific a study etymology is.

Etymology

ETYMOLOGY is the study of the origins of words. We have already seen (in Chapters 3–5) that we can borrow words from various places or create our own from English. With passing time, the origins of these words can become obscure. For instance, you could not guess by looking at it that the word *lord* was originally a compound word made up of the elements corresponding to modern English *loaf-ward* and meaning 'bread keeper' or that the word *lady* was originally a compound word made up of elements corresponding to *loaf-kneader*. Nor could we guess from the current form of the word that *pantry* has its origins in an Old French word meaning 'place for keeping bread'.

To discover these things, we have to consider when words first appeared in English, the ways in which words were used in earlier periods of English and the ways they were spelled. We also have to look at the words in languages from which the English might have been borrowed, or in which something which was originally the same word might have developed along similar lines. In these ways we find out about two different things: the way in which words have developed in English, and the ways in which cognates have devel-

Cognate

oped in related languages. COGNATES are words in different languages which share a common origin. English *bread*, Danish *brød*, Dutch *brood* and German *Brot* are cognates from four languages. In this case, they all mean 'bread'. Less obviously, perhaps, English *tale*, Danish *tale*, Dutch *taal* and German *Zahl* are cognates. The Danish means 'a speech', the Dutch means 'language' and the German means 'figure, number'. Despite the differences in meaning, all these words share a common origin, a form which we can guess must have been something like *talō in the language which was the common ancestor of English, Danish, Dutch and German (the asterisk here shows that the form is not known in its own right, but is RECONSTRUCTED from later forms). We will consider the ways in which words have changed their meanings in Chapter 11, while here we will be more concerned with showing what words are related to which others.

Reconstructed

EXERCISE ✎

10.1 Consider the following set of cognates from English and German. What do you notice about the differences in spelling?

English	German
tame	zahm
ten	zehn
tide	Zeit ('time')
toll	Zoll ('customs')
to	zu

Initial *t* in English corresponds regularly to initial *z* in German. It is because there is regularity in correspondences of this type that we can find cognates even when the meaning has changed in one or more of the languages concerned. While it can be very difficult for the inexperienced student to see regular correspondences in the form of words, it is possible to give a few fairly simple spelling rules which can help. For instance, there are a number of consonant correlations between the classical languages and the Romance languages on the one hand, and the Germanic languages (including English) on the other, which are reflected in words which are borrowed from these other languages. These are set out below:

Greek, Latin, French, etc.	English
p	f
t	th
c	h
d	t
g	c/k

The first three correspondences do not operate when there is a preceding *s-* in the same word. Instances where these correspondences show up are illustrated in the highlighted letters below:

paternal	father
heart	cardiac
genus	kind

Grimm's Law

This set of correspondences is usually known under the name of GRIMM'S LAW, after Jacob Grimm, who not only gets the credit for explaining this pattern, but was also one of the authors of Grimm's fairy tales.

EXERCISES ✎

10.2 The pairs of words below illustrate Grimm's Law. Mark the consonants which show the relevant correspondences. *Canine, hound*; *cannabis, hemp*; *cornucopia, horn*; *dental, tooth*; *genuflect, knee*; *nepotism, nephew*; *pedal/tripod, foot*; *Pisces, fish*; *pro-life, for*.

10.3 A Greek *h* often corresponds to a Latin *s*. Examples are Greek *hemi-* which is in origin the same root as Latin *semi-*, and *herpes* from Greek meaning 'a creeping illness', which corresponds to *serpent* from Latin. Find two other instances of this correspondence, and some English words which show it. (Hint: think of words for geometrical figures.)

10.4 Compare the following cognates from German and English. What do you notice about the initial *Pf* in German? Why should the German word for 'plant' have a *z* in it?

English	German
pan	Pfanne
path	Pfad
penny	Pfennig
pepper	Pfeffer
plant	Pflanze

Once you know something about the origins of English words, you can start to see some very interesting patterns, where English uses words which have their origins in Germanic languages and words which have their origins in French and Latin, but which have very similar meanings. For instance, if we consider a word like *forerunner*, we can divide that into three morphemes (see Chapter 7), *fore· run(n)·er*. *Fore* means 'before', *run*, obviously, means 'run' and *-er* means 'agent', or the person who performs the action. Now consider the word *precursor*. *Pre-* is Latin for 'before', *curs-* is a Latin root meaning 'run' and *-or* is the Latin agent marker, so that *precursor* and *forerunner* are based on precisely the same picture, but one has a Germanic origin, the other a Latin origin. In another case, though, *fore·bear* literally means 'to carry before' and the Latin translation element-by-element yields *pre·fer*, which does not have the same meaning in English at all.

EXERCISE ✎

10.5 Here are some Latin roots and their meanings. *Cede* 'to go'; *dic* 'to say, tell'; *face* 'to speak, a word'; *lude* 'to play'. Given these meanings, which of the following words forms pairs with Germanic words like *forerunner*, and which form element-by-element translations like *forebear*? *Precede, predict, preface, prelude*.

Further study reveals that there are many words which at first glance have little to do with each other which are, nevertheless, related etymologically. Once this is pointed out, it is sometimes possible to see a vague connection in meaning, although even that is sometimes difficult.

EXERCISE ✎

10.6 Each of the following sets of words are related etymologically. What meaning links them? Which letters carry that meaning?

    (a) *direct, regal, regular, rule*
    (b) *cellar, conceal, hell, supercilious*
    (c) *kin, genus, pregnant, germ*

Despite the number of words whose origins we can discover by careful study in this way, there are always some whose origin remains obscure even to the most committed searcher after word-origins. In dictionaries these words frequently merit no more than a curt remark such as 'etymology dubious', although the suggested histories may be fascinating. Such a word is *loo* meaning 'toilet'. There are a number of possibilities which have been suggested by various authorities.

1. *Loo* is the name of a card game which was current in the seventeenth century. It seems unlikely, however, that there is any connection here.

2. *Loo* or *lew* is a West of England dialect word meaning 'a sheltered spot', and is related to the standard English word *lee*. If this is correct, the extension of meaning here is fairly clear.

3. It comes from the French word *l'eau* 'the water', either
    (a) as a kind of ironic reply to the French name for a toilet, *les waters*, or
    (b) from the phrase *gardez l'eau* or *gardy loo* which was common in Edinburgh at the time of the major French influence on Scotland. This is the phrase people would shout as they emptied their night buckets out of the windows of high tenement blocks into the street below. The phrase means 'mind the water', which was a bit of a euphemism. Again the connection is fairly easy to see.

4. It comes from the French phrase *lieux d'aisance*, which might best be translated with the American English expression 'comfort station'.

5. It comes from the continental habit of marking toilet doors with the symbol 'OO'. The initial *l* would be a mock French definite article. A similar derivation is found in the tennis term *love* which comes from the French *l'oeuf* 'the egg', because a zero looks like an egg.

6. It comes from a pun on *Waterloo*. Again there may be some connection the French expression *les waters*, or with the English word *water closet*. Apparently there is also an attested French usage of *Waterloo* meaning 'buttocks'. Although it does not, strictly speaking, prove anything, the following segment from James Joyce's *Ulysses* is usually cited in support of this theory:

> Oh yes, mon loup. How much cost? Waterloo. Water-closet.

It is the last derivation which current opinion favours, but the facts are still not absolutely clear. This example makes the point that there is a difference between knowing the etymology of a word and having some plausible-sounding story as to where it might have originated.

EXERCISE ✎

10.7 Look up the word *loo* in a dictionary which provides etymological information. Compare the amount of information you are given there with the discussion above. What do you learn about dictionary etymologies?

In cases like this – and also in cases where the etymology *is* clear to the specialist, it must be said – it is frequently true that stories about the origins of words gain currency in the community. Frequently these stories are demonstrably false, yet people are sure that they know the etymology of the word in question. A case in point is the etymology of the word *sirloin*, which is commonly believed to have been so noble a cut of beef that it was knighted by a king. In fact, the *sir* part is a mis-spelling for French *sur*, and it means 'the part above the loin'.

In other instances there may not be the same picturesque stories about the origins of words, but false beliefs about their structure are obvious from the form they acquire. In these cases, the technical term for the false etymology is FOLK ETYMOLOGY. Some examples will make the point. *Asparagus* has a dialectal form *sparrow grass*, where the unfamiliar and opaque structure of the original has been given a (false) meaning. Similarly, the word *cockroach* comes from the Spanish *cucaracha*, and has no connection with either *cocks* or

Folk etymology

roaches. A *bridegroom* has no connection with a *groom* who looks after horses; rather the form originates from the Old English form *guma* meaning a 'man', and became opaque when that word ceased to be used on its own. A word which is currently acquiring a folk etymology is the word *utmost* as in *to do one's utmost*. This is frequently written (and almost invariably pronounced) as *upmost*. *Up* means something, while *ut* does not.

EXERCISE ✎

10.8 Each of the following words has a form due to folk etymology. What is the real origin of the word? Why has it been re-analysed? *Hang-nail, humble pie, terrapin, Welsh rarebit, woodchuck.*

FOLLOW-UP READING

The etymology of *loo* is discussed in A. S. C. Ross, 'Loo'. *Blackwood's Magazine* 316 (1974), pp. 309–316, which is also an extremely good and clear source on the difference between folk etymology and scientific etymology. For investigations into etymological matters, *The Oxford English Dictionary* is an absolute necessity. More manageable than this, though, is *The Oxford Dictionary of English Etymology*, which will probably be found useful for some of the exercises. Discussion of Grimm's Law can be found in any book that deals with the history of English or with historical linguistics in general (e.g. Jean Aitchison, *Language Change: Progress or Decay?* Cambridge: Cambridge University Press, 1991), although coverage is not as lucid as one could wish in all such books. Also, the coverage here has been modified to deal with *spellings* rather than *sounds*.

11 WORDS THAT CHANGE THEIR MEANINGS

In this chapter we look at words whose meanings have changed markedly, sometimes several times, and sometimes so drastically that we can scarcely recognise them any more.

When the Teenage Mutant Ninja Turtles described good things as *awesome*, they were helping along a process that has been going on as long as language has existed: they were helping a word change its meaning. *The Oxford English Dictionary* lists the earliest meanings of *awesome* as 'inspiring awe' and 'dreadful'. That is, the earliest meanings of *awesome* referred to things which made you feel awe because of how terrible or weird they were. Today, *awesome* has become a word descriptive of just the opposite state of affairs: things that are *awesome* are wonderful, superb, terrific, neat. According to *The Oxford English Dictionary*, this meaning is first found in the 1980s. Words which describe things as being very good or very bad are often words which change their meanings rapidly, because over-use of a particular word makes it feel weak and a new hyperbole is required.

EXERCISE ✎

11.1 Can you guess by looking carefully at the words what *awful*, *terrific* and *wonderful* once meant?

If we know enough about the etymology of a word, we can frequently find it changing its meaning several times. The word *silly* is cognate with (see Chapter 10) Danish *salig* and German *selig*, both of which mean 'happy' though the Danish is more likely to mean happy for religious reasons, and the German may mean happy because of drunkenness. In English it meant 'deserving of pity' in the fifteenth century, 'ignorant' in the sixteenth century and then developed to mean 'foolish', as it does today.

EXERCISE ✎

11.2   Why should the meaning of *silly* change from 'ignorant' to 'foolish'?

A word which shows a similar development is the word *nice*. We can trace it back to Latin words *ne* and *scire* meaning 'not' and 'know', so that in origin it looks as though it meant 'ignorant'. From there it went on to mean 'foolish' in thirteenth-century English. This follows the same line of development as *silly*. From there, however, its history is very different. We can speculate that very fine distinctions were seen as being foolish, and so nice came to mean 'very fine, subtle or minute' in phrases like *a nice distinction* (which can sometimes still be found in legal works). It also came to mean 'dainty', and from there, 'generally agreeable' as it means today. It did not acquire this meaning until about the eighteenth century, yet at the beginning of the nineteenth we find Jane Austen commenting on its overuse for anything pleasant, in a way that continues to the present day. (The passage is cited in exercise 2.7.)

EXERCISE ✎

11.3   What would you say to someone who claimed that *nice* 'ought to mean' or 'really means' 'very fine, subtle or minute'?

Occasionally you can see some good reason for a change of meaning. For example, the word *rubber* used to be used to mean 'eraser' in New Zealand varieties of English (as in British varieties), but was rejected in favour of *eraser* once *rubber* came to mean 'condom'. This kind of embarrassment has also led people in many parts of the English-speaking world to stop calling the male of the domestic fowl a *cock*, preferring *rooster* instead, and has been suggested as the reason that *ass* was replaced by the word *donkey* in everyday usage.

Some people seem to feel that recent changes in meaning are unacceptable, and that words ought to mean what they used to mean. This is called the ETYMOLOGICAL FALLACY. It is simply not true that words must mean what they meant in previous generations, as we have already seen in this chapter. Words change their meaning when users of the words believe them to have a different meaning. Note, too, that people who make such claims rarely want words to go all the way back to their original meanings, they just want them to go back to the meaning that was around in a previous generation.

Etymological fallacy

This is only a relative conservatism. No one would seriously try to suggest that a sentence like *You are very nice because you don't know what the capital of Belgium is* really makes sense in present-day English.

EXERCISE ✎

11.4   Which meaning of *nice* would be captured in the sentence above if it made sense?

In general terms, the fact that words have changed their meanings over the generations does not cause us a great deal of trouble. It is true that when we read authors from earlier periods, we occasionally have difficulties understanding them. But such difficulties are typically brief, and seldom really important.

EXERCISE ✎

11.5   Which word in each of the following brief passages seems to have changed its meaning since the passage was written?

> Thy head is as full of quarrels as an egg is full of meat.
> (Shakespeare, *Romeo and Juliet*, III.i.20)

> And when I brought out the baked apples from the closet, and hoped our friends would be so very obliging as to take some, 'Oh!' said he directly, 'there is nothing in the way of fruit half so good, and these are the finest looking home-baked apples I ever saw in my life.' [. . .] And I'm sure by his manner, it was no compliment.
> (Jane Austen, *Emma*, Ch. 27)

> And he commanded us to preach unto the people, and to testify that it is he which is ordained of God to be the judge of quick and dead.
> (Acts X.42)

Although different dialects of English frequently show words with slightly different meanings – usually indicating that the word has changed its meaning in at least one of the dialects concerned – this does not usually cause us problems. We know that what the British call the *bonnet* of a car, the Americans call the *hood*, that British roads have *lorries* driving on them, while American ones have *trucks*, that *biscuits* are usually sweet for people from the United Kingdom but savoury for people from the United States, and so on. Occasionally we may be caught out by such a pair, but we don't find this offensive, even if we find it odd.

11.6 Can you translate the following terms into your own variety of English? They all concern items of clothing. If you are British, take the following terms to be American, and say what the British equivalent is. If you are American, assume that these terms are British, and translate into American. If you come from anywhere else, ask what these terms mean for you, and what other possible words there are for these things. *Jumper*, *knickers*, *pants*, *suspenders*, *vest*.

Occasionally, terms which have one meaning in one dialect and a different meaning in another dialect do give offence, though. An example is *learn*. In some dialects you can only learn something from someone; in others you can both learn something from someone, but also learn someone something (so that they end up knowing it). Speakers of the first kind of dialect sometimes find it objectionable when they hear the second kind. They want the second meaning to be covered by the verb *teach* instead. Another pair which works in much the same way is *lend* and *borrow*.

11.7 Each of the verbs below concerns transfer of something from one person to another. Call the person who has the object in the first place the Source, and the person who ends up with it, the Goal. For some verbs, the subject of the verb may only be the Source, for others, only the Goal, and for others, either. Which verbs behave in which ways? Is there any real confusion in the use of the verbs that can have either Source or Goal as their subject? *Buy*, *sell*, *lend*, *borrow*, *hire*, *rent*, *lease*, *charter*.

Arguments against using *learn* for both perspectives on this transaction are usually based on logic: there are two different activities involved, and so we need two different words. But this doesn't really hold up. I can hire a car from you or you can hire a car to me, and we use the verb *hire* independent of who is the instigator of the action. I can rent a car from you or you can rent it to me. The direction is made perfectly clear by the prepositions or other grammatical structures: *I'll learn you to cook an omelette* and *I learned to cook an omelette from her* are unambiguous. The real problem here is the social status of the people who speak dialects of this kind. There is plenty of evidence that people react to different dialects on the basis of their personal evaluations of the kind of people who speak those dialects, rather than in terms of the linguistic features of the dialects.

EXERCISE ✎

11.8   There are at least two different dialects of English with regard to the words they use ending in *-self*. Dialect A has the forms *myself*, *yourself*, *himself*, *herself*, *ourselves*, *yourselves* and *themselves*; Dialect B has the forms *myself*, *yourself*, *hisself*, *herself*, *ourselves*, *yourselves*, *theirselves*. Which dialect do you prefer? Why? What is the generalisation about how you know what to put before *-self* or *-selves* in the two dialects?

Some speakers find new meanings for old words offensive. You may have met this attitude from your parents or teachers, or you may not be aware of such feelings in the community, but they are there. You probably do not have such feelings yourself if you are under twenty-five, because you are too young to be aware that you are using new meanings of words, but in another forty or fifty years you will probably experience these same feelings yourself. I shall give just two brief examples.

Some people make a difference between the meanings of *uninterested* and *disinterested*, while others do not. *Uninterested* used to mean the opposite of *interested* in a sentence like *He is not interested in sailing* while *disinterested* used to mean the opposite of *interested* in a sentence like *She is an interested party in this dispute*. So in this dialect, *uninterested* meant 'bored', while *disinterested* meant 'impartial, unbiased'. *Disinterested* has now changed its meaning, though, for many speakers, so that it also means 'bored'. Speakers who make the distinction can be heard saying that speakers who do not make it (usually younger speakers) are losing an important distinction.

EXERCISE ✎

11.9   In a sentence like *I am totally disinterested in chess*, is it clear which meaning is involved? Can you make up any sentences in which it would not be clear which meaning is involved?

For many years, purists have been complaining about people who write things like *The noise rose to a crescendo*. In such sentences, they say, *crescendo* means 'a peak of loudness', while *crescendo* 'really' means 'a gradual increase in loudness'. According to such people, the *crescendo* is the process leading to the peak, rather than the peak itself. This is certainly the way the term *crescendo* is used in music. But the word appears to have acquired a new meaning as well – one closely related to the old meaning, but still distinct from it.

This process is inevitable. Words get new meanings. And we can no more stop using *crescendo* being used to mean 'peak of loudness'

than we can stop *silly* being used to mean 'foolish'. The only difference between the two cases is how recently the changes have taken
place.

12 DICTIONARIES

> In this chapter we ask how dictionaries are constructed and what they contain, with a view to giving you more realistic expectations about what a dictionary can do for you. We also see how editing a dictionary involves taking decisions on the matters that have been discussed in earlier chapters.

Dictionaries are the ultimate word-books, and often are associated with some of the magic of words, in that 'the' dictionary (as if there were only one!) is often assumed to be infallible. In Figures 12.1 to 12.3, brief extracts from three dictionaries are presented. In each case the section of the dictionary starting at the word *ding* and ending with the word *dingy* is given. One of the dictionaries is Australian, one is American and one is British. We shall refer to them simply as **MD**, **OD** and **MW**.

EXERCISE ✎

12.1 What nationality dictionary do you think is illustrated in each of Figures 12.1 to 12.3? Why?

In what follows, we will compare these three extracts from different dictionaries with a view to considering the ways in which dictionaries in general differ from each other and resemble each other. If you are choosing a dictionary for your own use or evaluating different dictionaries, you can use these questions to help you decide which dictionary is most likely to suit your purposes.

Word-list

First, then, we can see that some dictionaries have more words in them than others – they have a longer WORD-LIST – or they have different words in them. In some cases the differences are related

ding /dɪŋ/, *v.i.* **1.** to strike or beat. **2.** to sound, as a bell; ring, esp. with wearisome continuance. *–v.t.* **3.** to cause to ring, as by striking. **4.** to hammer at someone with repetitious talk. **5.** *Colloq.* to smash; damage. *–n.* **6.** a blow or stroke. **7.** the sound of a bell or the like. **8.** *Colloq.* a damaged section on a car, bike, surfboard, etc. **9.** *Colloq.* a minor accident involving a car, bike, surfboard, etc. [imitative]

dingbat /'dɪŋbæt/, *n. Colloq.* **1.** an eccentric or peculiar person. **2. the dingbats, a.** delirium tremens. **b.** a fit of madness or rage.

dingbats /'dɪŋbæts/, *adj. Colloq.* peculiar; odd; crazy.

ding-dong /'dɪŋ-dɒŋ/, *n.* **1.** the sound of a bell. **2.** any similar sound of repeated strokes. **3.** a loud and vigorous argument. *–adj.* **4.** repeated in succession or alternation. **5.** *Colloq.* vigorously fought with alternating success: *a ding-dong contest.* [imitative]

dinghy /'dɪŋgi/, *n., pl.* **-ghies. 1.** a small rowing or sailing boat or ship's tender. **2.** an inflatable rubber boat carried by aircraft, for use in emergencies. Also, **dingey, dingy, dinky.** [Hind. *dĩngi*]

dingo /'dɪŋgoʊ/, *n., pl.* **-goes, gos,** *v. –n.* **1.** the Australian wild dog, *Canis familiaris dingo,* introduced by the Aborigines, often tawny-yellow in colour, with erect ears, a bushy tail and distinctive gait, and with a call resembling a howl or yelp rather than a bark. Also, **native dog. 2. a.** a contemptible person; coward. **b.** one who shirks responsibility or evades difficult situations. *–v.i.* **3.** to act in a cowardly manner. **4. dingo on (someone),** to betray (someone). *–v.t.* **5.** to shirk, evade, or avoid; to spoil or ruin. [Aboriginal]

dingy /'dɪndʒi/, *adj.,* **-gier, -giest. 1.** of a dark, dull, or dirty colour or aspect; lacking brightness or freshness. **2.** shabby; disreputable. [orig. uncert.] – **dingily,** *adv.* – **dinginess,** *n.*

Figure 12.1 **MD.**[1]

directly to the aims of the dictionaries, such as the fact that the **MD** contains more Australian words. In some cases the difference is related to the overall size of the dictionary (the **MD** is the smallest of the three dictionaries considered here), something which is usually related to the retail price of the dictionary. It is often the case that a longer word-list correlates with a less clear TYPOGRAPHY or layout: here we see that the information from **MW** is harder to read, but more information is given. Other policy decisions affect the length of the word-list: although it is not clear from these extracts, **OD** includes abbreviations in its word-list, while **MW** does not. We see here that **OD** also includes foreign phrases.

Typography

When you read claims about dictionaries on their dust jackets, any claims about the number of words covered usually involves counting all the words in bold face. Note that **MD** has two entries for *dingbat* and *dingbats*, while **OD** has only one. You might like to consider whether **MD** really has one more word here than **OD**. The problem for dictionary editors (as, in a rather different way, for people trying to estimate vocabulary size: see Chapter 2) is translating lexemes into headwords: when do derivatives and compounds, for instance, need to be new headwords, and when can their meanings be deduced

[1]Taken from *The Macquarie Concise Dictionary,* 2nd edn., The Macquarie Library Pty Ltd, 1988.

ding[1] /dɪŋ/ v. & n. ● v.intr. make a ringing sound. ● n. a ringing sound, as of a bell. [imitative: influenced by DIN]

ding[2] /dɪŋ/ n. Austral. slang a party or celebration, esp. a wild one. [perhaps from DING-DONG or WINGDING]

ding-a-ling /'dɪŋəlɪŋ/ n. **1** the sound of a bell. **2** N. Amer. an eccentric or stupid person.

Ding an sich /ˌdɪŋ an 'zɪx, German 'zɪç/ n. Philos. a thing in itself. [German]

dingbat /'dɪŋbat/ n. slang **1** N. Amer. & Austral. a stupid or eccentric person. **2** (in pl.) Austral. & NZ **a** madness. **b** discomfort, unease (gives me the dingbats). [19th c., in early use applied to various vaguely specified objects: perhaps from ding 'to beat' + BAT[1], influenced by BAT[2], BATTY]

ding-dong /'dɪŋdɒŋ, dɪŋ'dɒŋ/ n., adj., & adv. ● n. **1** the sound of alternate chimes, as of two bells. **2** Brit. colloq. an intense argument or fight. **3** Brit. colloq. a riotous party. ● adj. (of a contest etc.) evenly matched and intensely waged; thoroughgoing. ● adv. Brit. with vigour and energy (hammer away at it ding-dong). [16th c.: imitative]

dinge /dɪn(d)ʒ/ n. & v. ● n. a dent or hollow caused by a blow. ● v.tr. make such a dent in. [17th c.: origin unknown]

dinghy /'dɪŋgi/ n. (pl. -ies) **1** a small boat carried by a ship. **2** a small pleasure boat. **3** a small inflatable rubber boat (esp. for emergency use). [originally a rowing boat used on Indian rivers, from Hindi ḍīṅgī, ḍĕṅgī]

dingle /'dɪŋg(ə)l/ n. a deep wooded valley or dell. [Middle English: origin unknown]

dingo /'dɪŋgəʊ/ n. (pl. -oes or -os) **1** a wild or half-domesticated Australian dog, Canis dingo. **2** Austral. slang a coward or scoundrel. [Dharuk din-gu or dayn-gu 'domesticated dingo']

dingy /'dɪn(d)ʒi/ adj. (**dingier**, **dingiest**) dirty-looking, drab, dull-coloured. □ **dingily** adv. **dinginess** n. [perhaps ultimately from Old English dynge DUNG]

Figure 12.2   **OD.**[2]

from general principles? Are affixes to be treated like words (and given a headword to themselves) or not?

EXERCISES ✎

12.2   You will sometimes hear claims of the type 'that's not a word, it's not in the dictionary'. How would you respond to this kind of claim for a form like dinge, for instance, on the basis of **MD**?

12.3   Consider the number of 'words' with the form ding and ding-dong that are listed in each dictionary. What kind of effect could this

[2]Taken from the Oxford Concise Dictionary, 9th edn., 1989, by permission of The Oxford University Press.

¹ding \'diŋ\ *vb* [prob. imit.] *vt* (1582) : to dwell on with tiresome repetition ⟨keeps ∼*ing* it into him that the less he smokes the better —Samuel Butler †1902⟩ ∼ *vi* **1** : to make a ringing sound : CLANG **2** : to speak with tiresome reiteration

²ding *n* [*ding* (to strike), fr. ME *dingen*] (ca. 1945) : an instance of minor surface damage (as a dent)

ding–a–ling \'diŋ-ə-,liŋ\ *n* [redupl. of ¹*ding*] (ca. 1935) : NITWIT, KOOK

ding·bat \'diŋ-,bat\ *n* [origin unknown] (1904) **1** : a typographical symbol or ornament (as *, ¶, or ✠) **2** : NITWIT, KOOK

¹ding·dong \'diŋ-,dȯŋ, -,däŋ\ *n* [imit.] (1611) : the ringing sound produced by repeated strokes esp. on a bell

²dingdong *vi* (1659) **1** : to make a dingdong sound **2** : to repeat a sound or action tediously or insistently

³dingdong *adj* (1792) **1** : of, relating to, or resembling the ringing sound made by a bell **2** : marked by a rapid exchange or alternation

dinge \'dinj\ *n* [back-formation fr. *dingy*] (1846) : the condition of being dingy

ding·er \'diŋ-ər\ *n* [perh. fr. *ding* (to strike) + ²-*er*] (1974) : HOME RUN

din·ghy \'diŋ-ē, -gē\ *n, pl* **dinghies** [Bengali *diṅgi* & Hindi *diṅgī*] (1810) **1** : an East Indian rowboat or sailboat **2 a** : a small boat carried on or towed behind a larger boat as a tender or a lifeboat **b** : a small sailboat **3** : a rubber life raft

din·gle \'diŋ-gəl\ *n* [ME, deep hollow] (13c) : a small wooded valley : DELL

din·gle·ber·ry \'diŋ-gəl-,ber-ē\ *n* [origin unknown] (1955) : a piece of dried fecal matter clinging to the hair around the anus

din·go \'diŋ-(,)gō\ *n, pl* **dingoes** [Dharuk (Australian aboriginal language of the Port Jackson area) *diṇgu*] (1789) : a reddish brown wild dog (*Canis dingo*) of Australia

din·gus \'diŋ-(g)əs\ *n* [D or G; D *dinges*, prob. fr. G *Dings*, fr. gen. of *Ding* thing, fr. OHG — more at THING] (1876) : DOODAD 2

din·gy \'din-jē\ *adj* **din·gi·er; -est** [origin unknown] (ca. 1736) **1** : DIRTY, DISCOLORED **2** : SHABBY, SQUALID — **din·gi·ly** \-jə-lē\ *adv* — **din·gi·ness** \-jē-nəs\ *n*

dingo

Figure 12.3 **MW.**[3]

have on publicity claims about coverage of the dictionaries? What system determines how many words are listed in each dictionary?

Definition

Next we find that many of the words in the word-list have a DEFINITION (though not every word in bold type is defined; look at *dinginess* and *dingoes* in all three dictionaries). Writing dictionary definitions is a highly skilled task. The definitions have to be succinct, accurate, comparable with definitions of other related words in the dictionary, they must avoid circularity (if the definition of word *x* uses word *y*, the definition of *y* must not presuppose that you understand *x*), and above all, they must be understandable. It frequently seems that some of these requirements are mutually incompatible, but the good lexicographer (or dictionary-writer) pays attention to all of them. Synonymy and hyponymy are regularly used as strategies for providing definitions. The lexicographer also has to decide when meanings are distinct enough to make it desirable to treat one form as having two headwords (i.e. as homonyms), and when words should be treated as polysemous.

[3]By permission from Merriam-Webster's *Collegiate® Dictionary*, 10th edn. © 1996 by Merriam-Webster, Incorporated.

EXERCISES ✎

12.4 Write a definition of a word such as *chair* or *table* as if for a dictionary. Do not look it up in any dictionary before you begin! If possible, have someone else criticise your definition, by asking questions such as 'Would this definition fit a stool, a sofa, a bench, etc.?' If your definition becomes more than a couple of lines long, try to shorten it while keeping it accurate and comprehensible.

12.5 Below are listed the definitions from *The Concise Oxford Dictionary* (9th edition) for the following words: *crabby, gloomy, glum, morose, sulky, sullen, surly*. Which definition belongs to which word? What is your conclusion about the definitions given?

- bad-tempered and unfriendly; churlish.
- depressed; sullen.
- irritable, morose.
- looking or feeling dejected, sullen; morose.
- morose, resentful, sulky, unforgiving, unsociable.
- sullen and ill-tempered.
- sullen, morose or silent, esp. from resentment or ill temper.

Pronunciation

Each of the dictionaries provides a representation of the PRONUNCIATION of the word. **MD** and **OD** both represent the pronunciation by using the symbols of the International Phonetic Association (although the two transcriptions are not identical), while **MW** uses only a few such symbols, and prefers to use English letter-sound correspondences, especially for the vowel sounds. Lexicographers rarely worry about alliteration, rhyme or phonaesthemes, but information about morphemes may be derivable indirectly from their entries.

Grammatical information

Each of the dictionaries also provides a minimal amount of GRAMMATICAL INFORMATION, restricted to the part of speech and whether verbs are intransitive or transitive. Dictionaries aimed at foreign learners of English usually give a lot more grammatical information.

Style label

Many dictionaries also give STYLE LABELS for words, showing whether they are informal, slangy, etc. Such labels always have to be treated with some suspicion: one dictionary marked both *cabby* ('taxi-driver') and *cunt* as 'informal', yet there are times when the first can be used but not the second!

Illustration

Many dictionaries also provide some ILLUSTRATIONS. In some these illustrations take the form of line drawings or plates, but such things are expensive, and useful for only a limited number of words. More common, especially in recent dictionaries, is the use of illustrative phrases, showing you how a particular word is used and what collocations it appears in. Such illustrative phrases are perhaps particularly common in dictionaries which are aimed at people learning English as a second or foreign language, but they are also useful for native speakers of English, who may have come across a word in one context, and not know precisely how it can be used in another context. **MW** makes a point of giving genuine examples of usage (see the entry for ¹*ding*, for example), and line drawings. The other dictionaries use invented phrases to illustrate usage (see under *ding-dong* in **OD**). **MW** also provides as a matter of course synonyms or near-synonyms (in small capitals), and in some entries (not shown in the entries given here) distinguishes between such near-synonyms.

EXERCISES ✎

12.6 Consider the following words. Which of the types of illustration discussed above might be helpful in a dictionary for someone who was looking these up? *Akimbo, blonde, crimson, definite article, mizzen mast.*

12.7 In Figure 12.4 are entries for *tranquillize* from two dictionaries from the same publisher. The first is from *The Collins English Dictionary* (3rd edition, 1991), the second from *Collins COBUILD English Language Dictionary* (1987) which is aimed at non-native speakers of English. The two dictionaries differ in, among other things, the way in which they provide grammatical information and the number of illustrative phrases they provide. In many cases *COBUILD* provides much more grammatical information. Does it do so here, and if so what does it tell you that the *Collins English Dictionary* does not? What do you think the symbol '⇑' means? How does the illustration help your understanding?

> **tranquillize, tranquillise,** *or U.S.* **tranquilize** ('træŋkwɪ͵laɪz) *vb.* to make or become calm or calmer. —͵**tranquilli'zation,** ͵**tranquilli-'sation,** *or U.S.* ͵**tranquili'zation** *n.*

> **tranquillize** /træŋkwɪlaɪz/, **tranquillizes, tranquillizing, tranquillized**; also spelled **tranquillise**. American English also uses the spelling **tranquilize. 1** If you **tranquillize** a person or an animal, you make them become calm, sleepy, or unconscious by giving them a drug. ᴇɢ *He chartered a plane, tranquillized the bears, and flew them 500 miles north.*
>
> V+O : USU PASS ⇑ sedate

Figure 12.4, From *The Collins English Dictionary* and *Collins COBUILD English Language Dictionary*

All three of these dictionaries give some information on the etymology of the words discussed – their origins and development. This section is frequently difficult to understand because it contains many abbreviations, references to other languages, and tends to make very fine distinctions which may not be immediately obvious, distinctions such as 'from', 'taken from' and 'cognate with', for instance. Etymology has been discussed in Chapters 10–11, and will not be considered further here. One point is absolutely crucial though: you must never confuse the etymology of a word with its meaning.

EXERCISE ✎

12.8   Consider the etymology given for *dingy* in the three dictionaries. In the light of the discussions in Chapter 10, can you interpret the information you are given?

There are other aspects of dictionaries which are not illustrated in the brief extracts illustrated here. For example, all dictionaries have to deal with multiple-word lexical items, from compounds which are written as two separate words to IDIOMS such as *kick the bucket* and *bite the dust* (both meaning 'die'). **MD** lists, among many others, the following combinations with the word *long*: *in the long run*, *the long and the short of it*, *long in the tooth*, *before long*, *as long as*, *long division*, *long-eared bandicoot*, *long johns*, *long jump*, *long-sighted*, *long weekend* and *longwinded*.

Idiom

Finally, many dictionaries have appendices containing various kinds of information, some of which is part of the ordinary word-list of other dictionaries. With these, as with the other aspects of dictionaries that have been mentioned, you have to know how the dictionary you are using works to get the most out of it. Read the introductory material to your dictionary, and see how its editors think you should use it!

What we have done in this book is consider the issues which have to be faced by dictionary-makers. That is why the chapter on dictionaries provides a conclusion to the book.

WHERE NEXT?

13

Here are some suggested readings to carry on your study of vocabulary.

In considering vocabulary, we have looked at words from several different angles, and you may be interested in following up particular lines of enquiry that have been considered in this book. In some chapters (e.g. Chapter 1), the references given at the end of the chapter are sufficient to allow you to do this. But you might want to go on to consider the history of English words in particular, lexical semantics (the meanings of words), morphology (the ways words are built up and created), lexicology and lexicography (the study of dictionaries and how to write them), or even other areas which have not been discussed in this book. Here I suggest some books you might like to look at next in considering these areas.

To study the history of English in particular and the etymology of English words, you will need a good history of the English language. There are many such books available. One which I personally like is Barbara M. H. Strang, *A History of English* (London: Methuen, 1970). A now rather old-fashioned book, but still interesting in its discussion of vocabulary, is Mario Pei, *The Story of the English Language* (London: Allen and Unwin, 1968). David Crystal, *The Cambridge Encyclopedia of the English Language* (Cambridge: Cambridge University Press, 1995), which is an excellent all-round work on the English language, contains a section specifically on etymology. *The Oxford English Dictionary* and one of the several available etymological dictionaries will be necessary for any serious study of the origins of English words.

On lexical semantics, the best book is D. A. Cruse, *Lexical Semantics* (Cambridge, etc.: Cambridge University Press, 1986).

On morphology there are now a number of good works, including my own *Introducing Linguistic Morphology* (Edinburgh: Edinburgh University Press, 1988), or, more up-to-date but more specialised, Francis Katamba, *Morphology* (Basingstoke: Macmillan, 1993). On the use of classical elements in the construction of English words and the interpretation of the resulting words, Keith Denning and William R. Leben, *English Vocabulary Elements* (New York and Oxford: Oxford University Press, 1995) is recommended.

Despite its title, Leonhard Lipka, *An Outline of English Lexicology* (Tübingen: Niemeyer, 1990) covers many of the matters that have been dealt with in this book and is not limited to the study of dictionaries in any narrow sense. Lexicology has been given rather more attention by French specialists than by English-speaking ones, and most of the English-language discussion is quite technical. Tom McArthur, *Worlds of Reference* (Cambridge: Cambridge University Press, 1986) is interesting in that it sets dictionaries in a wider context. Various entries in Tom McArthur, *The Oxford Companion to the English Language* (Oxford and New York: Oxford University Press, 1992) relate to dictionaries of different kinds.

If you are interested in onomastics (the origins and meanings of names), you will have to consult some of the many dictionaries of personal names or place names. Crystal's *Encyclopedia of the English Language* is probably the best introductory text on the subject. There is also an entry in McArthur's *The Oxford Companion to the English Language*.

If you are interested in how our minds manipulate and store words, then read Jean Aitchison, *Words in the Mind* (Oxford and Cambridge, Mass.: Blackwell, 2nd edition, 1994).

For swearing and slang, see Lars Andersson and Peter Trudgill, *Bad Language* (Oxford: Blackwell, 1990).

For sheer fun, try Gyles Brandreth, *The Joy of Lex* (New York: William Morrow, 1980 or later editions) and *More Joy of Lex* (New York: William Morrow, 1982).

And, for all dealings with words, arm yourself with at least one good dictionary (you will probably end up wanting to consult several!) and a good thesaurus, and find out how to use them properly.

ANSWERS TO EXERCISES

These are suggested answers for the exercises which appear throughout the book.

1.1 The obvious examples are cases of blasphemy, using the names of deities in inappropriate circumstances. This is even written into law, although the laws are rarely applied these days. This is very similar to the case of the Chinese emperors, since emperors are, in many cultures, treated as quasi-deities.

1.2 The implication of the behaviour reported in this story is that if the word *sack* is not used, being sacked will not be as hurtful to the person involved; since it is the action of sacking which is the real attack on the person, the words used should make no difference, though they clearly do.

1.3 Again, the implication is that the word is just like the thing, or the word is in some sense the same as the thing. Interestingly, some of these taboos are very culture specific. You may speak another language where the same problems do not arise (though similar ones will).

1.4 To be intoxicated: you can be *inebriated, intoxicated, drunk, pissed, smashed, blotto,* and so on; consult your thesaurus for another forty or so near-synonyms. Some of these relate to degrees of intoxication, others are simply used in different circumstances. You would be unlikely to tell a judge that anyone had been *pissed as a newt*. To evacuate the bowels: *to defecate, to move one's bowels, to have a motion, to relieve oneself, to shit*. Compare also the near-synonyms *faeces, stools* and *turds*. To pass wind: *to suffer from flatulence, to break wind, to fart*. To die: *to be no more, be deceased,* *pass away, pass over, meet one's maker, snuff it, kick the bucket, pop one's clogs, turn up one's toes.* Not all of these words and phrases are precise synonyms, and some of them are rather jokey in tone, but it still remains the case that some of them are permissible in one set of circumstances, but not in others.

1.5 *Touch wood, keep your fingers crossed, cross my heart (and hope to die), bless you!* [said in response to a sneeze], *white rabbits* [said on the first on the month], and so on.

1.6 Some words are clearly viewed as being too offensive (that is, as having too much power) to be let loose on number plates – even if they are not properly spelled!

CHAPTER 2
Vocabulary
Statistics

2.1 The answer is provided in the following text.

2.2 The lexeme GO has the following word-forms: *go, goes, going, went, gone.* BE has more: *am, are, is, was, were, be, being, been. Important* and *many* have only one word-form each. But nouns and verbs generally have more than one form.

2.3 The *lie* in (2) belongs to the same lexeme LIE as is illustrated in the earlier citation from *The Tempest*: both are verbs, and both mean 'to be in a recumbent posture'. The *lie* in (1) is a noun, not a verb, and means 'falsehood'. The *lies* in (3) is a separate lexeme again: it is a verb and means 'to tell falsehoods'. Words in different parts of speech are nearly always said to belong to different lexemes, even if they have the same form. Words with radically different meanings also belong to different lexemes (different dictionary words).

2.4 Here is a list of the words in the passage with some notes. The smallest possible number is 52, the length of the list. The largest number is 64, counting each possible difference as a separate word. The point of the exercise is to make it clear how much difference counting different things makes to the final score, even in such a short text.

a (x3)	fool (x2)	it
am (x2), be, is	for (x3)	lie (x2); it is not
and (x7)	foul	clear whether
but (x3)	have, hath	they both mean
by (x2)	heaven	'tell lies'
defiles, defile	her (possessive, x3),	light
do (auxiliary verb,	her (objective)	love (x2)
main verb)	here (x2)	melancholy
down	I (x6), me	(adjective, noun)
eye (x2), eyes	in (x3)	my (x3)

not	so (x2)	(verb)
nothing	sorrow	two
O	taught	well (sentence
of	that	adverb x2,
part	the (x3)	adverb)
pitch'd (verb), pitch	thee	wit
(noun x2)	they (x2)	word
proved	this	world
rhyme (noun, verb)	throat	would
say (x2), said	to	yes
set	toil (noun), toiling	

2.6 There are a number of possibilities. One is just that school brings you face to face with a host of new technical words you never use outside the classroom. Part of the answer is probably that learning more words makes it easier to learn even more: if you know *photograph* and *claustrophobic*, it is easier to work out what *photophobic* must mean. People who do not start learning early enough – perhaps because they learn another language first – may continue to learn words at speed longer than others, and people who miss out on exposure to appropriate words at the usual stage may learn them later, perhaps less easily.

2.7 Perhaps *interesting* for 'a book', *fine* for 'a day', *invigorating* for 'a walk', *attractive* for 'two young ladies' and *useful* for 'a word'.

2.8 The two words are *contemporary* and *text*. *Current* and *writing* would be possible alternatives that are in the Longman list.

2.9 The words changed in the first text are, in order: *plumage, maintenance, bedraggled, unable, predators, preening* and *scratching*. The words from the second text are *startling, panting, sweated, flicked, bellies, hind* and *hoofs*. You probably find it more difficult to guess what the missing word means (a) when there are several such words close together, (b) where the context seems to allow any one of a number of solutions and (c) in the more academic text. But this is the way you learn new words, so if you heard the words often enough, you would be able to work out something of what they mean. You may well have found words which mean the same as the word that was changed, but was not just the same word, e.g. *enemies* instead of *predators*. In terms of this exercise, such words provide good answers, because they show that you *can* predict the meanings of words. We will discuss such words, called SYNONYMS, in Chapter 6.

3.1 You will have discovered that the question is really asking if you knew or could guess where the foods and animals originated. The correct answers are listed below – and some of them are very tricky.

CHAPTER 3
Borrowing

Words borrowed	Source language	Spoken in
barbecue	Haitian via French	Haiti
bouillabaisse	French	France
chocolate	Aztec via Spanish	Mexico
curry	Tamil	India
frankfurter	German	Germany
molasses	Portuguese	Portugal
moussaka	Greek	Greece
paella	Spanish	Spain
smorgasbord	Swedish	Sweden
spaghetti	Italian	Italy
tea	Chinese	China
tomato	Aztec via Spanish	Mexico
coyote	Aztec via Spanish	Mexico
gnu	Xhosa	South Africa
jackal	Persian via Turkish	Persia
jaguar	Tupi-Guarani	Paraguay, Brazil, Bolivia
kangaroo	Guugu Yimidhirr	Australia
kiwi	Maori	New Zealand
macaw	Portuguese	Portugal, Brazil
mammoth	Russian	Russia
merino	Spanish	Spain
orang-utan	Indonesian	Indonesia
springbok	Afrikaans	South Africa

3.2 Italian has prestige particularly in the field of Italian cookery (because that is where it comes from) with words like *lasagne*, *minestrone*, *tortellini*; music (because of the strong influence of renaissance Italian music) with words like *adagio*, *allegretto*, *piccolo*; and art (because so many famous artists of the Renaissance were Italian), with words like *chiarascuro*, *fresco*, *torso*. French has prestige in many areas of cookery (because cookery was developed into a real art in France) with words like *cuisine*, *éclair*, *roux*; and in women's fashion (because so many of the leading fashion designers in the late nineteenth and twentieth centuries were French), with words like *bustier*, *chemise*, *negligée*.

3.3 *Artisan*, *marry* and *noble* are French, they deal with legal status; *gift* and *skill* are Scandinavian, they are everyday words.

3.4 *Taboo* is from Tongan and *mana* is from Maori, both languages of Polynesia. All the little, grammatical, words are native English, but none of the content words are. This would not necessarily be the case in a text about more everyday matters.

4.1 Compounds within compounds have been marked off with square brackets:

> The [Web browser] wars have heated up again with the release of the platform preview of Internet Explorer 4.0 and the third preview version of [Netscape] Communicator. . . .[F]eatures include an intelligent web searcher and a new search 'pane' which lets users see [search engine] results and web pages at the same time

4.2 *Catgut* 'B is part of A' or 'B comes from A', like *sheepskin*; *claw hammer* 'B has the feature A' like *paperback book; dog biscuit* 'B is for A' like *cat flap*; *doormat* 'B is at place A' like *hearth rug*; *health farm* 'B is the place where you go for A' like *restroom* (although *restroom* is a euphemism); *health food* 'B is used for the sake of A' – I can find no parallels to this one, but perhaps you can; *teaspoon* 'B is used for A' like *soup spoon*.

4.3 My source for this compound is the following: 'Rainy days, . . . the sliding doors that led to the deck were crawling with rain-snakes' (Ed McBain, *Cinderella* (London: Hamish Hamilton, 1986), p. 223). So rain-snakes were things that look like snakes and are made out of rain. Your suggestions may be just as possible, e.g. snakes that appear in wet weather.

4.4 People who love pets hit by a global panic in scare involving the discovery of rabies in bats.

Britons on holiday in scare caused by disease.

Weddings rejected for people who have had operations to change their sex.

Accident during a run to get into training puts paid to brave battle for fitness.

If we simply count in numbers of words we have almost doubled the number by removing compounds.

4.5

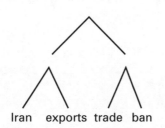

Iran   exports   trade   ban

**CHAPTER 5
New Words
from English 2:
Derivatives**

5.1   The affix means something like 'do the opposite of' (e.g. if you disconnect two things, you do the opposite of what you do if you connect them). The words containing the prefix are *disconnect*, *discontinue*, *disengage*, *disinfect*, *disorder* and *displease*. *Disaster*, *diskette*, *discuss* and *distress* do not contain the affix. If *discuss* did contain the affix, it would have to mean 'do the opposite of cussing', which is not what *discuss* means.

5.2   There may be difficulty in deciding where the affixes begin and end, but even with words like *anti·dis·establish·ment·ari·an·ism* you should not find any more than in the examples already given.

5.3   Try *parental*. *Parentalise* means 'make parental' (you may never have heard the word before, but what does that matter?). Can you imagine someone saying *I want to parentalise control over the children* meaning 'I want the control to be provided by the parents'? What about *parentalisation*? It means 'the act or fact of making parental'. Perhaps, *His parentalisation of the control failed to give the expected benefits*. What then about *parentalisational*? This means 'to do with parentalisation'. *Parentalisational control is not a new option*. But now we need to ask whether this is different from *Parental control is not a new option*. *Parentalisationalise* means 'to make to have to do with the act or fact of making parental'. I can't think of a case when that would be useful, but perhaps you can. In my experience, words stop making sense with about this number of affixes – which presumably is why we don't usually have more.

5.4   The three trees are as follows:

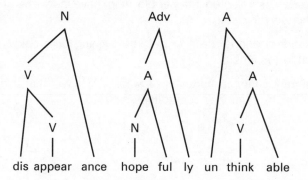

The problem with *undoable* is that it is ambiguous, and has two different structures, one corresponding to each meaning. If you put *un* and *do* together first it means 'able to be undone', and if you put *do* and *able* together first it means 'not able to be done'.

5.5   Although these few words are not sufficient to tell you how English works in general, you should have found that *un-* is only attached to adjectives. There are other *un-* prefixes with different meanings which attach to other parts of speech (*unlock*, *unperson*, *unplug*, etc.), but this one does seem to be restricted to adjectives.

5.6 With verbs ending in *-ate* you have to add *-ion*, and with verbs in *-ify* you have to add *-cation* (changing the '*y*' to an '*i*' as you go), as in *translate*, *translation* and *justify*, *justification*. Even if you thought up brand new verbs with these suffixes, they would have to form nouns in that way.

5.7 It suggests that the affix *-ese* is productive in English. I would expect it to sound fine to describe the language of teachers as *teacherese*, or the language of students as *studentese*. The existence of other words on the same pattern should confirm the notion that this affix is indeed productive.

CHAPTER 6
Meaning
Relationships

6.1 While *pail* and *bucket* can both be used of the same entity sometimes, *pail* cannot be used to describe the scoop in a dredger or excavator, in the phrase *kick the bucket* meaning 'die' or as a measure in *it was raining buckets*. *Torch* and *flash-light* differ in that the first is a British expression equivalent to the second American expression, in some places the two are distinguished in terms of style (a *flash-light* being the kind of thing you buy from an expensive shop, while *torch* is the ordinary word) and you cannot put *flash-light* in place of *torch* in *carry the torch for someone*.

6.2 *Big* has the antonym *little* (or *small*) and *polite* has the antonym *rude* (or *impolite*). *Borrow* is not an adjective, and neither is *son*, so they do not have antonyms in this specialised sense. *Dead* has an 'opposite' *alive*, but this is not a gradable distinction: anything which is not dead is alive. Only if you think there are degrees of deadness and aliveness is *alive* an antonym of *dead* in this sense.

6.3 *Animal* is a bit like *dog*. You might think that *animal* is a super-ordinate term for *insect*, or you might think that *animal* excludes *insects*, etc. So you may have an answer like the following:

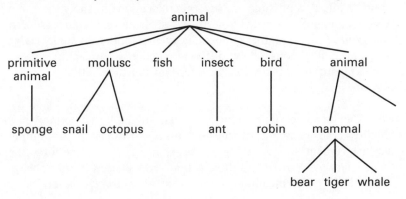

6.4   The diagram below shows the relationships:

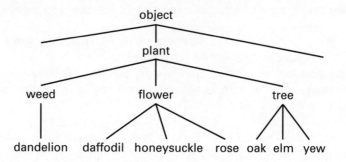

6.5   Your answer will depend upon the terms you have found. You will have some general level (basic) colour terms like *red*, *yellow*, *blue* which will all be incompatible with each other. You will also have some terms which are hyponyms of these basic terms, like *crimson*, *scarlet*, *mauve*, *heliotrope*, *violet* and so on. You will probably find it easier to define the basic colour terms by making reference to other basic terms, and to define the hyponyms of these in terms of their own relationships. There will be some terms, such as *turquoise*, which may appear at one level or the other, depending on your own attitude to these labels.

6.6   You should find at least the following: *snow*, *sleet*, *slush*, *hail*, *ice*, *drift*, *icicle*, *iceberg*, *pack ice*, *snowflake*, *snow shelf*. While some of these do seem to match the Eskimo terms – as far as we can tell from the definitions – others do not, and we do not have any ordinary word for 'rotten snow on the sea'. We must therefore conclude that the two languages do divide up their experience of the world differently.

6.7   *Hard* collocates with *case, cash, copy, core, decision, disk, feelings, frost, hat, labour, look, luck, man, question, rock (music), way, work,* and with other nouns as well. *Ground* collocates with *to break, to gain, to give, to lose* and with *common, firm, high, holy, soft* and so on. While it is possible for several collocations to show the same basic meaning of the word you are considering (e.g. *gain*, *give* and *lose ground* all treat the same military metaphor), in many cases different collocations show different shades of meaning of the original word: *hard disks* and *hard feelings* illustrate different meanings of *hard*.

6.8   The meaning of *-ness* in *cheapness* might be something like 'quality'; the meaning of the *-er* in *dish·wash·er* is something like 'instrument'; the meaning of the *-ee* in *pay·ee* is something like 'beneficiary' or 'patient' (although that term is used in many ways in linguistics); the meaning of the *-ic* in *photograph·ic* is probably no more than 'adjective'; the meaning of the *-ise* in *visual·ise* may be something like 'make' or 'causative' or 'transitive verb'. You may have found more specific answers; in that case you need to ask whether your answers will generalise to other uses of the same affix.

7.1 As we saw in Chapter 2, since one of the *shed*-words is a noun and the other a verb, they must belong to different lexemes. Their different meanings also provide an indication.

**CHAPTER 7
Formal
Relationships**

7.2 *Polish* can mean 'of Poland' or 'a waxy cleaning preparation' as in *car polish*. I cheated by putting it first in the sentence, so that it got a capital letter. These are homographs but not homophones. *Bare* is a homophone of *bear*; *bear* 'an animal' and *bear* 'carry' are homographs and homophones. *Common* can be the opposite of *rare* or a public place in the middle of a village; these are homographs. *Cuff* can be a noun or a verb, again homographs and homophones. *Supply* can be a noun or a verb, but it can also be the adverb corresponding to *supple* (a word which can also be spelled *supplely*). In this last case it is not a homophone but is a homograph. *Two* has a homophone *too* (and possibly *to*, as well).

7.4 In order: pig, mouse, duck, horse, sheep, cow, cat, dog.

7.5 Opinions will differ, but a possible answer is 'none'. It is not always easy to tell precisely which words do contain a given phonaestheme.

7.6 In (a) *glass* and *glaze* may not contain the phonaestheme, but the others are related to light in some way. There seems to be general agreement that there is a phonaestheme here. We might argue about *jump* and *lump* in (b), but the others probably contain a phonaestheme, with a meaning something like 'a dull sound'. The words in (c) were chosen at random from a dictionary, and are not supposed to contain a phonaestheme, though you might have found meanings in common between some of the words concerned.

7.7 {pre}, {determine}, {d} – the morphemes appear in *pre-pay*, *determines* and *loved*; {press}, {ure}, {s} – you might not think that *pressure* can be divided into meaningful elements, but my analysis here is based on parallels such as *closure, departure, exposure*, etc. and the other morphemes appear in *presses* and *cats*; {undulate}, {s} – the morphemes appear in *undulated* and *loves*; {un}, {friend}, {ly} – the morphemes appear in *unlikely*, *friendship* and *matronly*.

7.8 In spelling, {in} becomes *il-* and *ir-* as in *illegal* and *irrelevant* respectively. In pronunciation, you can hear only one /l/ or /r/ sound, so we can say that the prefix is reduced to just the vowel.

7.9   The letter *g* is pronounced as /g/ in the longer of each pair of words (when there is an affix on the end), but not when the *g* followed by an *n* or an *m* is at the end of a word. (This is not the absolute rule, because of forms like *signing* with no /g/ sound; only some affixes bring out the /g/.) There are also changes from long vowel sounds to short vowel sounds in the first two pairs. *Sign* is not written as *sine* because that would lose the connection with *signature* and other similar words (*signal*, *signatory* etc.). There are various places where English spelling prefers to keep the same morpheme spelled the same way despite its pronunciation, rather than to reflect the pronunciation accurately. The plural marker discussed in the text is one other.

CHAPTER 8
Stylish Words

8.1   The poem is 'Twinkle Twinkle Little Star'. The choice of words, especially obsolete words like *aster* and *vivific*, creates a large part of the effect of this version of the poem. However, the word-order in *Fain would I* and the order of noun and adjective in *gem carbonaceous* add to this effect. In other texts the use of subordinating conjunctions like *although*, *after*, *when* etc. instead of the co-ordinating conjunction *and* would have the effect of increasing the formality level. Your version of 'This is the House that Jack Built' might contain, for instance, 'This is the domesticated mammal of the genus *Canis* that pursued the domestic feline mammal that apprehended the rodent of the genus *Rattus* that consumed the germinated and dried cereal that was situated in the domiciliary edifice erected by John.'

8.2   (a) (association) football; (b) vocabulary or word-formation; (c) flying or planes; (d) chemistry; (e) ballet. Note that the vocabulary in effect defines the subject matter. Also note that the same word can belong to more than one subject area.

8.3   You will probably find that different generations use different words, and people from different schools may also use different words. If you have people in your group who have come from different schools, you might compare your lists. Or get your parents or grandparents to tell you what they said when they were your age. If you need further inspiration, look in a thesaurus. If your parents used the words from your generational group they would probably sound rather ridiculous to your ears.

8.4   I got up this morning, brushed my 'Amstead 'Eath (teeth) and my Barnet Fair (hair), kissed the dustbin lids (kids) and put on my tit for tat (hat) to go for a ball of chalk (walk) up the frog and toad (road). I didn't have much bees and honey (money), but I still put an Oxford scholar (dollar = 25p) on a Charing Cross (horse) that came in at 20 to 1. I could hardly Adam and Eve (believe) my Donald Duck (luck)! So I went to the rub-a-dub (pub) and had a pig's ear (beer) with some china plates (mates). Only one, though, because I didn't want to be elephant's trunk (drunk) [less politely, Brahms and Liszt] when I got home to the trouble and strife (wife).

8.5 *Get off, go up, go away, put away / lock up, tell off.*

8.6 My suggestions are presented below. The first version would probably be more suitable for a children's book, the second for a technical work.

> On Io, the **gravitational** pull of the three nearby moons is enough to change the shape of the world itself, making it throb with a heartbeat-like *lub-dub*. This throbbing <u>movement</u> churns up heat inside the moon, which in turn stirs up moonwide **volcanoes**. Though such otherworldly outbreaks are thrilling, they are little more than fireworks made with earth and stones.

> On Io, the **gravitational attraction created** by the **proximity** of a <u>trio</u> of **satellites** is **sufficient** to **distort** the <u>structure</u> of the <u>celestial</u> body itself, <u>causing</u> it to **pulsate** with a **cardiovascular periodicity**. This RHYTHMIC **motion creates internal** THERMAL ENERGY, which **consequently generates extensive volcanoes**. Though such <u>PHANTAS-MAGORICAL</u> **erupting** is DRAMATIC, it <u>amounts</u> to <u>mere</u> GEOLOGICAL PYROTECHNICS.

CHAPTER 9
Technical Words

9.1 For example, other words containing the element *tele-* include the following: *telegraph, telepathy, telephoto, teleport, telescope.* Other words containing the element *phon(e)* include: *dictaphone, gramophone, homophone, hydrophone, megaphone, phonetics, phonics, phonograph.*

9.2 'Distance'; 'sound': see the following text.

9.3 *The Oxford English Dictionary* defines *geophone* as 'A device or instrument used to detect vibrations such as sound-waves or shock-waves in the ground.' You should have got as far as 'earth-sound' if no further. It might be possible for it mean 'sound created by the earth', for example.

9.4 *Phot(o)* means 'light' and is found in *photocopy, photoelectric, photograph, photon, photosynthesis*; *hydr(o)* means 'water' and is found in *hydraulic, hydrogen, hydrology, hydrolysis, hydrophobia*; *(o)logy* means 'study of' and is found in *archaeology, biology, ecology, geology, zoology*; *psych(o)* means 'mind' (in classical Greek it meant 'soul') and is found in *psychedelic, psychic, psychiatry, psychology, psychotic.*

9.5   *Leucodendron*, *leuchaemia* (which you may know with the alternate spelling *leukemia*) and *leucanthous*. These are all English words.

9.6   *Aquaphobia* links with *aqueduct*, *aquamarine*, *aquifer*, *aquarium*, *Aquarius* etc. where the link is with water, and means 'fear of water'. *Brontophobia* you can deduce only if you know the literal meaning of *brontosaurus*, a 'thunder lizard' because of the noise it is supposed to have made moving around; *brontophobia* means 'fear of thunder'. *Gymnophobia* is a trick question – you will recognise the link with *gymnast*, *gymnasium* etc., but probably do not know that these received their name because Greek athletes competed naked in a gymnasium. There are technical words like *gymnorhinal* meaning 'having naked or unfeathered nostrils', and *gymnophobia* means 'fear of nudity'. The *log(o)* element in *logophobia* you may recognise from *logorrhea*, and also in *catalogue*, *dialogue*, *travelogue*, *astrologer*, *philology*, all of which are linked by 'speech' or 'words'; *logophobia* means 'fear of words'. *Necr(o)* occurs in *necromancy*, *necropolis*, *necrosis*, and in its Latin version in *internecine*; it has to do with death and corpses, and *necrophobia* is 'fear of corpses'.

CHAPTER 10
Where Words
Come From:
Etymology

10.1   The answer is provided in the following text.

10.2   **C**anine, **h**ound; **c**annabis, **h**emp; **c**ornucopia, **h**orn; **d**ental, **t**oo**th**; **g**enuflect, **k**nee; **n**epotism, **nephew**; **ped**al/tri**p**od, **f**oot; **P**isces, **f**ish; **pro**-life, **for**.

10.3   Latin *sex-* versus Greek *hex-* 'six' as in *hexagon*; Latin *sept-* versus Greek *hept-* 'seven' as in *heptagon*.

10.4   German initial *Pf* corresponds to English initial *p*. Note that the word for 'pepper' shows that something else happens in other places in the word. The *z* in *Pflanze* is a generalisation of the rule we saw in exercise 10.1.

10.5   *Precede* and *forego* are element-by-element translations that do not mean the same; *predict* and *foretell* mean the same thing; *preface* and *foreword* mean the same; *prelude* and *foreplay* are used in different contexts, though both are anticipating the main event.

10.6   *Direct*, *regal*, *regular*, *rule*: other related words include *royal*, *regulation*, *regent* etc. The original fundamental meaning was 'rule', and royal persons of all kinds rule or direct others. If something is *regular* it conforms to a rule in a slightly different sense of *rule*, but one which still has the same source. The only relevant letter found in all these words in English is *r*, but we can trace most of them back to Latin *reg*. *Cellar*, *conceal*, *hell*, *supercilious*: all of these contain a fundamental meaning of hollow or enclosed space. *Hollow* is also related (try Grimm's Law!). *Supercilious* comes from *super* 'above' and *cilium* 'eyelid', the eyelid being the part which CONCEALS the eye. What is above the eyelid is the eyebrow, and haughtiness is supposedly seen in the attitude of the eyebrows. The letters carrying the meaning are the *c/h* and the *l*. Other related words are *hole*, *helm* (but not of a ship, which has a separate source) and *helmet*. *Kin*, *genus*, *pregnant*, *germ* all contain the idea of begetting, as do the related *gonads*, *gonorrhoea*, *ingenious* etc., where the *k/g* and *m/n* are the letters that carry that meaning.

10.7 You will certainly not get the degree of discussion that was given here, only an answer or the correct, but not very helpful, remark that the origin is unknown or obscure. By making a choice, dictionary writers (a) take the chance of being wrong and (b) hide much of the really interesting material.

10.8 *Hang-nail* was originally *ang-nail* or 'pain-nail'. It also over-hangs, and when *ang* disappeared, it was reinterpreted as *hang*. *Humble pie* was originally *umble pie*, where *umble* means 'offal'; presumably you were thought to eat umble-pie only out of humility. *Terrapin* has nothing to do with either *terra* or *pins*, coming from a native American word *turepé*. *Welsh rarebit* was originally called *Welsh rabbit* (in the same way that rolled sheep-meat is called *colonial goose* in Australia and New Zealand). Since it clearly was not rabbit, it was assumed that the word must be something else. *Woodchucks* do not chuck wood at all. The word is originally from the Cree language, and is *wuchak*, but *woodchuck* is fairly close in sound and means rather more.

11.1 *Awful* used to mean 'full of awe, inspiring awe', *terrific* used to mean 'causing terror' and *wonderful* used to mean 'full of wonder, inspiring wonder'. *Awful* and *wonderful* look as though they may have meant precisely the same at one stage, though they were specialised in more or less the present senses very early in the history of English. *Terrific* now means just the opposite of what it once meant.

CHAPTER 11
Words That Change Their Meanings

11.2 There is a very deep-seated assumption that if someone does not know something it is because they are incapable of learning things, although there is no necessary link between the two. It is hardly surprising, then, that a word should move from meaning one to meaning the other.

11.3 I hope you'd laugh at them! This answer is explained in the following text.

11.4 The earliest, 'ignorant'.

11.5 An egg could not be said to be full of meat in today's English, but in Shakespeare's time *meat* just meant 'food' (compare the phrase *one man's meat is another man's poison*, where the same meaning is retained, however little we are aware of it). It seems quite clear that the comment on the baked apples *is* a compliment in our understanding of the word, but for Austen it meant 'flattery, an empty compliment'. The word *quick* used to mean 'alive'. The same meaning arises in *His fingernails were bitten to the quick* (i.e. to the living flesh) and in *quicksands*.

11.6

If you are British, the British equivalent of the American word in the middle is:		If you are American, the American equivalent of British word in the middle is:
pinafore dress	jumper	sweater
knickerbockers	knickers	panties
trousers	pants	underpants, shorts
braces	suspenders	garters
waistcoat	vest	undershirt

11.7 *Sell* and *lend* have the Source as the subject: *She lent me her notes*. *Buy* and *borrow* have the Goal as their subjects (at least in standard varieties of English): *I borrowed the notes from her*. *Hire*, *rent*, *lease* and *charter* allow either Source or Goal as their subjects, apparently without any confusion.

11.8 You probably prefer Dialect A, but may not know why. If you tried to explain this in terms of beauty or logic, you are almost certainly wrong. There is no generalisation to help you decide what to put in front of -*self* or -*selves* in Dialect A; in Dialect B, though, you always put the possessive word that you would use in *They wanted Kim to buy ___ car* (*my, your, his, her, our, your, their*). Dialect B is thus more consistent. The real difference is that Dialect A is a standard dialect, while Dialect B is not.

11.9 It should be clear that the meaning is 'bored'. It is very difficult to find cases where you might be in doubt as to which meaning is intended, which makes the point that having two meanings for the same form *disinterested* is not a major problem for speakers.

CHAPTER 12
Dictionaries

12.1 Figure 12.1, labelled **MD**, has the excerpt from the Australian *Macquarie Concise Dictionary* (2nd edition). You can tell because of the number of different (local) uses of the word *dingo*, and because it does not mark *dingbats* as being Australian. Figure 12.2, labelled **OD**, is the excerpt from the British *Concise Oxford Dictionary* (9th edition), which specifically marks *dingbat* as being Australian or North American. Figure 12.3, labelled **MW** is from the

American *Merriam Webster's Collegiate Dictionary* (10th edition), and if you look at the pronunciation for *dinger*, you will see it is pronounced with an /r/ on the end. Neither standard British nor standard Australian English has such a pronunciation.

12.2   *Dinge* is not in **MD** but is in the other two dictionaries (albeit with different meanings, so we might want to claim that two distinct lexemes DINGE are represented). The fact that *dinge* is not in **MD** is related to the overall size of that dictionary as compared with the other two: its word-list is constrained by the size of the dictionary. Clearly, then, we cannot make any absolute decision about the existence or otherwise of a word if the size of the dictionary we are searching is the final arbiter of our conclusion. Only if we had a dictionary which listed every word ever used anywhere (and you will see with a little thought that this is impossible) could we make such claims.

12.3   We can see that one dictionary has two words *ding*, while the others have one; that one has three entries for *ding-dong* while the others have one. A superficial count of **MW** might conclude that it had more words than the others simply on the basis of instances like *ding-dong* if there were enough of them. Only a very careful comparison would allow us to decide which dictionary actually contained more information. **MW** has a different entry for every part of speech (noun, verb, adjective). The others do not do this, though they may have two entries if they think the meanings are completely unrelated.

12.4   Check the definitions given by a number of different dictionaries. Are they suitable or is yours better?

12.5   *crabby*: irritable, morose.
   gloomy: depressed; sullen.
   glum: looking or feeling dejected, sullen; morose.
   morose: sullen and ill-tempered.
   sulky: sullen, morose or silent, esp. from resentment or ill temper.
   sullen: morose, resentful, sulky, unforgiving, unsociable.
   surly: bad-tempered and unfriendly; churlish.

The more successful you are in associating the correct word with the correct definition, the more likely you are to be impressed with the skill of the dictionary-writer, and the more likely you are to think that the dictionary suits you.

12.6   A line illustration of someone with arms akimbo would be very helpful, but so would a note that *with arms akimbo* is virtually the only phrase in which the word occurs (I have once seen someone described as having legs akimbo, and couldn't understand what was meant!). *Blonde* does not denote a precise colour, so there would be no point in putting it on a colour chart, but very few things are described as *blonde*: people, hair (wigs, moustaches, etc.) and wood (or things made with it). *Crimson* can perhaps only be described with a colour chart or by listing objects which are typically crimson. The definite article is the word *the*, which is by far the easiest way of defining it. A *mizzen mast* is more easily shown on a picture than described, although it can be described.

12.7 As well as giving the word-forms of the lexeme TRANQUIL-LIZE, the COBUILD dictionary tells you explicitly that the verb is transitive (takes an object) and is usually used in the passive. The CED implies that the verb can be either transitive or intransitive in its definition, but does not give information about the passive use. The symbol '⇑' means that the word next to it is a superordinate term for the headword. The illustrative phrase gives you no new grammatical information, but shows the kind of context the verb is likely to be used in.

12.8 While **OD** suggests a specific etymology for *dingy*, the others merely note that its etymology is uncertain. This is probably one of those cases like *loo* (discussed in Chapter 10) where there are several theories, and none is completely certain.

INDEX